Who Said What?

A Writer's Guide to
Finding, Evaluating,
Quoting, and Documenting
Sources (And Avoiding
Plagiarism)

Kayla Meyers
Foreword by Susan Wise Bauer

WELL-
TRAINED
MIND
PRESS

Publisher's Cataloging-In-Publication Data
(Prepared by The Donohue Group, Inc.)

Names: Meyers, Kayla, 1992- author. | Bauer, Susan Wise, writer of supplementary textual content.
Title: Who said what? : a writer's guide to finding, evaluating, quoting, and documenting sources (and avoiding plagiarism) / by Kayla Meyers ; foreword by Susan Wise Bauer.
Description: [Charles City, Virginia] : Well-Trained Mind Press, [2019] | Includes index. | Interest age level: 10 and up. | Summary: "A thorough, accessible guide to research, citation, and source evaluation, designed to assist students growing up in an era of changing media, fake news, alternative facts, and information overload"--Provided by publisher.
Identifiers: ISBN 9781945841422 | ISBN 9781945841439 (ebook)
Subjects: LCSH: Report writing--Juvenile literature. | Research--Juvenile literature. | Information literacy--Juvenile literature. | Bibliographical citations--Juvenile literature. | CYAC: Report writing. | Research. | Information literacy.
Classification: LCC LB1047.3 .M49 2019 (print) | LCC LB1047.3 (ebook) | DDC 371.30281--dc23

Portions of this guide are adapted from the *Writing With Skill* series by Susan Wise Bauer., copyright 2012, 2013, 2014 Well-Trained Mind Press.

Cover design by Mike Fretto
Typesetting by PerfecType, Nashville, TN.

www.welltrainedmind.com

CONTENTS

FOREWORD

I've been a writing teacher for decades, and I can testify: Writing is an incredibly hard skill to teach, because *writing is thinking.* When you're putting your words down on paper, you're putting your *mind* down on paper—and that's not a simple task.

When you're learning to write nonfiction essays and research papers, writing gets even more complicated. When you're writing well, you're not just setting down *your* thoughts—you're reading, thinking, and synthesizing the ideas that other people have had, combining them with your own, and repeating their ideas but then building on them to come up with new ones.

And while you're doing all of *that,* you also have to worry about giving credit where credit is due. In today's wired world, it is simply too easy for writers (even experienced professionals, as Kayla Meyers deftly highlights in Part 4, "How To Avoid Stealing") to accidentally plagiarize. Kayla recognizes this problem, and addresses it head-on with a set of practical suggestions, easily applied.

I've watched hundreds of young writers struggle with the complicated, overlapping rules about documentation—and often come to a dead stop because they simply can't get their heads wrapped around the problem. *Who Said What?* cuts right through the tangle, offering a clear, easy-to-follow set of principles. Not sure whether you need to footnote a statement or not? Kayla clears up the confusion. Not certain even *how* to footnote or endnote? Kayla's succinct directions will point you towards the answer. She walks students, step by step, through a process that is too often presented as overly complex: finding sources, taking notes, using those notes to construct a composition, and acknowledging where the ideas came from.

I first met Kayla when she began to teach writing for us at the Well-Trained Mind Academy, our classical online school. It was instantly clear that she had both rapport with her students, and a gift for straightforward, effective communication with them. She also grasped, very quickly, that they needed a simpler guide to the process of finding, using, and citing other authorities.

Kayla's experience as a young writer and teacher also highlighted something I'd underestimated: students need to know what a *reliable* (authoritative, mediated, genuine, non-fake) source *is*. When I was a beginning writer, I could look to books and magazines for information. Now, students can glean information from thousands of websites, from audiovisual archives, from social media sites, and from other resources that simply didn't exist twenty—or even five—years ago. Many of these sources are crowdsourced, "semi-mediated," unmediated, or just plain deceptive. Kayla offers clear, simple advice about how to distinguish the reliable from the faulty, inaccurate, outdated, or even maliciously twisted. And she also gives invaluable guidance for incorporating insights from social media (ever present!) into legitimate research.

Working with the principles and rules set out in my full-year curricula *Writing With Skill* and *Grammar for the Well-Trained Mind*, while drawing on her own experience and expertise, Kayla has put together this invaluable handbook for the writer-in-training. It's more than a reference—it's a quick-start guide for researchers, designed to get them reading and writing without delay.

Susan Wise Bauer

HOW TO USE THIS BOOK

You can, of course, read this book straight through, for a full explanation of how and why these skills of finding the right sources, researching, note-taking, citation, and direct/indirect quoting all fit together. But if you are in a hurry, you can jump to the section that is most relevant to what you need (or what part of the research process you are stuck on).

At the end of each section, you'll see a list of bullet-points summing up what you've just learned. At the end of each Part, there is a Quick Reference that lists all of the bullet-points from each section within. This Quick Reference provides a full summary of the Part.

Use these bullet-points to check your understanding after reading each section or Part—or as a resource anytime you need a quick refresher on the material!

The Index at the end of the book is also a great resource to help you locate and review specific terms.

Part 1
What Sources Are, and Where to Find Them

What are sources?

A research paper just wouldn't be a research paper without a hearty band of **sources** to back it up. Sources are simply the books, articles, websites, images, videos, etc. that you find, read (or view), and then take notes from as you prepare to write. Sources provide the information that you will ultimately use to formulate your ideas and support your claims in your original writing. The types of sources you find and use will be determined by your teacher's preferences and your paper requirements. But once you've decided on a clear, specific topic for your paper, finding sources is your next step.

Faced with a library of books, or even worse, the entire internet, you might find it difficult to know where to begin—and what a reliable source even looks like. But don't panic! This guide will walk you through the process of finding reliable sources—in a library or online—and give you guidelines on how to sniff out any suspect information.

- Sources provide reliable information that you will use to formulate your ideas and support your claims in a paper.
- Sources can be books, articles, videos, website content, and any other medium that provides information related to your paper topic.

How do I know if this source is reliable?

It would be great if you could perform a background check on every source and author you come across in your research! But that would be incredibly impractical, especially if you're on a tight paper deadline.

Instead, think of the information in your sources as fitting into two categories: **mediated content** and **unmediated content**.

Mediated vs. unmediated content

Mediated content has been edited and fact-checked for general accuracy by a third party, generally one who has a financial or academic stake in the work. Essentially, mediated content is any work that has had more than one person review and edit the information. This increases the chance that the source is reliable.

Keep your critical glasses on: Mediated content can still be biased, inflammatory, or just plain wrong. But because it is mediated, it is appropriate to cite as a source in your paper.

Unmediated content travels directly from the originator to the reader, without any other person filtering or checking the information. Personal websites, for example, are unmediated. Only the author has looked over the content! When you're writing a paper, unmediated content is not appropriate to cite as a reliable source.

It was once easier to determine what sources fit into which category. Books, for example, were traditionally mediated by editors and publishers. However, it has become so easy to self-publish that you can no longer assume a book is mediated, simply because it has covers and bound pages. And while websites were once primarily unmediated, now many reputable academic journals publish their content solely online.

Instead, you'll need to take on the responsibility of checking your sources closely to ensure that they contain mediated content.

Here are some questions to ask:

- Does the source have a clear publisher other than the author?
  - ▸ For websites, this could mean an institution that hosts the article and maintains the webpage (for example, the Smithsonian, or the Journal of Ancient History).
  - ▸ For books, this would be the name of the publishing house—but it's very easy to give your own self-publishing project an important name like Paramount Books, and some publishing companies, such as CreateSpace and Cafe Press, are actually platforms for self-publishing. Google the name of the publisher to make sure that it's an actual company with editors!
- Is the publisher or institution hosting the information well known? Do they have contact information available? Is there a corporate or institutional structure that you can look up—a president, CEO, board, etc.?
- Is the name of the author clear and easy to find? Is the author's contact information, or a biographical note for the author, provided? If you Google the author, what do you find out?
- Is the name of an editor (other than the author) available? If it is a website, is there a date for when it was last edited or updated? How recent is that date?

You don't need to have an answer for every question to prove that the source contains mediated content, but these questions serve as guidelines for you to test out the reliability of the source.

Finding mediated content begins at the research stage, and following good research procedures can help point you toward reliable sources. If you do encounter unmediated sources during your research, you can use the questions above to help weed them out.

Imagine that you're doing online research about the poem "The Tyger" by William Blake (we'll talk in the next section about how to do online research properly!). You come across two websites. One is mediated and the other is not. Can you tell the difference?

The first is hosted by Edublogs, and at the head of the page it simply says "English." The title of the essay is "Poetry Analysis: 'The Tyger' by: William

Blake." There's no author. The illustration is a stock photo of a bunch of brightly colored books, and the other menu options given are "Home," "College essay," "Mash-Up," "World Montage," and "Zen Podcast."

The second is hosted by the British Library. The title of the essay is "An introduction to 'The Tyger,'" the author is George Norton (you can click on his name to see the other essays he's written), and it was published on May 15, 2015. The illustration is of William Blake's original manuscript of "The Tyger." The main heading on the page says, "Discovering Literature: Romantics & Victorians," and your menu options are "Authors," "Themes," "Articles," "Videos," and "Teaching resources."

If you said that the first is unmediated and the second is mediated, you are correct! But how did you come to that conclusion?

You should have initially noticed that the first source has much less information available, making it impossible to answer many of the questions. There is no name given for the author of the piece, nor is there any information about when it was published. By contrast, the second source identifies the author and date of publication very clearly. Already you should have started growing suspicious of the first source.

What the two sources do share is a clear host institution: the first source is hosted by Edublogs and the second by the British Library. This may have answered the first question (Does the source have a clear publisher other than the author?) but it's the second question that is more revealing. Edublogs is not a well-known institution, and if you were to explore the webpage more, you'd have a hard time finding any reliable contact information. That is because Edublogs is a host platform for blog posts, but the company does not function as a fact-checking or editing institution. The British Library, however, is a well-known and reputable institution, with contact information easily accessible on the webpage.

Finally, the Edublogs website is clearly not set up to host serious and reliable academic work! Mistakes in punctuation such as "by: William" and random links to unrelated subjects suggest that this is either a personal website that hasn't been edited by an expert, or that the owner is trying to attract students in order to sell them papers (the "College essay" link leads to a place where you can buy essays online, which is dishonest and a violation of honor codes!).

Putting all of this information together, you should conclude that the post by the British Library is mediated, while the post on Edublogs is unmediated. As you can see, this decision is not made based on the content of the source necessarily, but on the available publishing and editing information.

Even if a website appears on the first page of your search return, always go through the process of checking whether a source is mediated or unmediated.

In the next section, I will explain more on how online search engines "think." But keep this in mind: Search engines do not give you, first and foremost, the sources that have the most factual information. They simply list first the returns that have received the most clicks in the past. So you have to do some detective work to determine if the source you have found contains reliable, factual information.

Let's return to my example search of "The Tyger." If I simply type "The Tyger William Blake" in the search bar, both the Edublogs and British Library pages appear on the first page. But so do many other sources of varying reliability and suitability, including pages from Shmoop, Sparknotes, and ThoughtCo.

These sites often fool students because they contain the type of analysis that would seem useful for a research paper. They also include a great deal of text. You might think: "If someone took the time to write so much on a subject, don't they know what they are talking about?" But never mistake wordiness for expertise! These sites, upon closer inspection, do not meet our requirements for mediated sources.

Like Edublogs, Shmoop and Sparknotes do not list a clear author or publisher. That is because these sites are **crowdsourced**. Crowdsourcing is when a large group of people, who may or may not have expertise on the subject, contributes information on a topic over the internet. Websites like Shmoop, Sparknotes, and Wikipedia rely on their readers to fill in and edit the site's content. Therefore, there is no formal publication process, and no knowledgeable editor who can mediate the information.

Sites like Yahoo Answers and Quora are also platforms where people can ask questions to the community of readers. The readers then vote on which answer is the "most helpful." These sites also frequently appear on the first page of a standard search engine. This voting process is much different than a formal fact-check that a reputable editor and publisher would do. Crowdsourced websites can simply be an accumulation of responses from people who really have no idea what they're talking about. (In fact, most of the people voting probably know even less than you do about the topic—they just thought the information would help them write a paper quickly!)

These crowdsourced websites also do not present their information in a reliable, trustworthy way. If I click on the Sparknotes and Shmoop links, my screen fills with advertisements. That's a clue! If you click on a website link and the information is partially obscured by many advertisements, that is a sign that the site is not purely informational, but intended to attract student clicks (for which the website earns money).

This brings us to ThoughtCo. ThoughtCo, unlike Shmoop and Sparknotes, has a clean website design and the names of the authors are clearly visible at the top. However, this is still not a reputable source. Like Edublogs, ThoughtCo is a blog-hosting platform, meaning that authors can write and self-publish their ideas without going through an editing process. So even though ThoughtCo appears more formal than Edublogs, it still is not a mediated source.

It is always better to use information provided by a well-regarded professional institution than to gamble on a website that only *appears* to be authoritative.

Determining whether a source is reliable is hard! In the next section, I'll explain how to approach online research so you can avoid crowd sourcing and blog-hosting websites. Even if you use news.google.com, which will return only news articles, it is difficult to know if the information provided in the article is true. But you are not alone in this! Fact-checking websites can help you determine fact from fiction, or even fact from exaggeration, when reading news stories. These websites use unbiased sources and neutral language to clarify and explain claims and issues that appear in the news. There are many well-regarded fact-checking websites, each with its own focus and expertise.

FactCheck.org is a non-partisan non-profit run by the University of Pennsylvania's Annenberg Public Policy Center. It monitors the factual accuracy of what politicians say in their speeches, press releases, TV ads, and even debates. They develop articles that explain contentious issues and clarify political statements.

Politifact.com is also a nonpartisan, non-profit organization that rates the accuracy of politicians' statements. They often put more emphasis on what is said over social media and what is current in the news, and use their Truth-O-Meter to rate political statements from "True" to "Pants on Fire," making fact-checks easily understandable to the public. Politifact also publishes the list of sources used to fact-check (when available) so readers can follow the organization's research.

Snopes.com is another respected fact-checking site, but functions differently than FactCheck and Politifact. Unlike the first two, Snopes tackles issues outside of politics and is usually the first to investigate rumors. However, Snopes determines what issues they investigate based on reader interest, so their coverage is not necessarily comprehensive.

ProPublica.org, though not a fact-checking website, is a non-profit, independent newsroom that supports investigative journalism. Their reporting covers a wide range of issues and is considered one of the most thorough fact-finding journalism websites.

These websites are essential research companions that will help you double-check the information that you find, especially in news sources. Many platforms make money off of clicks and shares on social media. These "fake news" sites will often bend, exaggerate, or even fabricate information to outrage readers. In such a research atmosphere, it is essential that you know how to tell the difference between legitimate and dishonest news sites. Fact-checking websites are unified by the goal of fighting misinformation and helping researchers, not gaining clicks, and can help keep your research focused on facts.

- Mediated sources are sources that have been fact-checked or edited by someone other than the author.
- Unmediated sources are sources that have not been fact-checked by a third party.
- You only want to use mediated sources for your research papers.
- Basic Google searches often return a mix of mediated and unmediated sources, so you will need to determine which sources are mediated and thus reliable for your research.

- Avoid crowdsourced or blog-hosting platforms, as they are not mediated.
- Do use sources from authoritative, well known institutions.
- Fact-checking websites (like FactCheck.org, Politifact.org, Snopes. com, and ProPublica.org) can help you verify information before you use false or exaggerated information in a research paper.

Can I use social media as a source?

The internet has not only expanded student access to information, but also diversified the mediums used to spread such information. These days, we are constantly plugged into social media, YouTube, and podcasts where we can quickly learn and share new things. Though these platforms may feel like genuine sources, they cannot be treated the same way as true, mediated sources.

While your instructor will determine what types of sources you can use for your papers, here is a general guide for how you should approach using social media, YouTube videos, and podcasts for academic research.

YouTube has become the center of learning for students. Want to learn how to cook an omelet? Need to review a math equation? YouTube is full of instructional videos that can help anyone master a skill.

When you are researching for an essay, though, you aren't simply trying to learn information as quickly as possible. Your goal is find and process that information, develop your own thoughts on the subject, and then explain those thoughts clearly in your own words. Most YouTube videos have been produced as crash courses on a topic, providing the information as simply as possible so a wide viewership can easily grasp it. So when you watch a YouTube video, you are absorbing the basic information, but are not doing the intellectual work necessary to develop your *own* ideas on a topic.

Some reputable institutions—such as the Smithsonian, the *New York Times*, and *National Geographic*—have produced excellent videos on a variety of topics. But even these videos have been crafted to maximize quick absorption, as opposed to providing detailed research on a topic. In these cases, it is always better to review the published articles by these institutions on the same subject for your research. Think of the YouTube videos as pointers towards published articles, rather than stand-alone sources.

YouTube videos not produced by well-regarded institutions have another issue: they are unmediated. Even if the producer claims to be an expert or enthusiast on the subject, YouTube has no fact-checking measure in place to ensure the information in the video is accurate. Since these videos are self-published, they are more similar to blog posts than the mediated, reputable sources we discussed earlier.

This same rule applies to posts on social media. Often, self-proclaimed experts will post their claims on Twitter, Facebook, or Instagram. No matter how well they argue their point, you should never blindly accept or cite social media posts as accurate. If you are interested in a point someone makes on social media, use authoritative sources and fact-checking sites to further investigate—and cite mediated sources, once you find them, instead.

Lastly, podcasts can fall into the same traps as YouTube videos and social media posts. Podcasts are often developed as sources of entertainment, and thus simplify or exaggerate information to appeal to broad audiences. Podcasts produced by journalistic institutions (like NPR or *The New York Times*) on current events are edited and fact-checked, so their information is more reliable. But producers often fail to mention or include their sources, even in the show notes.

For example, in July of 2019, the NPR and WBUR affiliated radio show "Here & Now" invited Nathan Daniel Beau Connolly and Edward Ayers, two historians who host their own podcast "Backstory," to discuss the history of regulating the tobacco industry. The historians used Sarah Milov's newly released book, *Cigarette: A Political History,* to research and develop their talking points for the show. However, when the segment aired, they failed to credit Milov or her book at all. Instead, over Twitter, Connolly gave her work a "shout out." It wasn't until the omission was publicized and critiqued that WBUR released a statement promising to add her name to the show notes. Even the most well researched podcasts sometimes fail to make their sources clear. So if you are a researcher, it is difficult to rely on the content of podcasts since you may not be able to trace where they found their information.

You're probably wondering, "So when can I use podcasts, YouTube videos, or social media in my research?"

You can use these types of sources when you are looking to quote someone to highlight their personal beliefs and opinions. For example, if I were writing a research paper on Brexit, I could use tweets from British politicians to highlight their opinions and feelings on the issue. I would not use their tweets as factual support – that is the job for reputable news and academic sources. It is essential to frame ideas expressed in social media posts, YouTube videos, and podcasts as the beliefs of the person expressing them. They should never be presented as objective fact.

- Social media posts, YouTube videos, and podcasts should not be treated in the same manner that you would approach reputable text sources.
- These mediums often over-simplify information, present opinion as fact, or fail to mention their own sources, making them unreliable for academic research.
- But social media posts, YouTube videos, and podcasts can be used to present the opinions or beliefs of individual people.

Where and how do I find sources?

Whether you are visiting your library or planning to do your research entirely online, start by reading an encyclopedia entry on your chosen subject. Depending on the scope of your subject, you may need to read a few encyclopedia articles. For example: if I am writing a paper on "Richard Nixon," I only need to read one entry on Nixon. But if my topic is more specific, say "Richard Nixon and the Vietnam War in 1968," I'll need to read additional encyclopedia entries on "the Vietnam War" and either "1968" or perhaps "the 1960s."

As you read through these entries, jot down important names, places, or ideas that relate to your subject. You will later use these as your search terms or **keywords**.

You may use a print encyclopedia or online versions of standard encyclopedias, such as *World Book* or *Encyclopedia Britannica*. I must caution you against using Wikipedia. Wikipedia is open for communal edits, and though there is a group of editors or "Wikipedians" who fact-check material and scan articles for incorrect or unfounded content, the process is imperfect and not immediate. So if you go to Wikipedia five minutes after someone has posted false facts (which many people do just for fun) you might write down incorrect information. Never use information from Wikipedia unless you've checked it with another source—and never cite Wikipedia as a source in any paper!

Once you have your keywords and basic facts on your subject written down, it is time to start hunting for your sources. Whether you head straight for the library or your computer will depend on your teacher's preferences and requirements, but I'll walk you through how to navigate both efficiently.

Using the library

Libraries have made themselves more accessible in the last decade, as many sources that you can find in your local library's stacks are available in digital formats. Libraries also have a reference section where you can typically find information from standard reference works and encyclopedias on thousands of different topics, but you cannot check reference books out of the building. Those sources will come up in an online search, but keep in mind that you will need to take time to visit the library to gain access to them.

So before you plan your library visit, start your research on the website's homepage. Whether a source is digitized or only available on a shelf, its information will still be included in the online catalogue, so searching the catalogue before your visit can give you a sense of what books or articles they have available for you.

Most library websites will have an easy-to-find search function for their catalogue. This may appear as a search bar in the middle or top of the page, but more advanced search options can be accessed through "Catalogue Search" or "Library Catalogue" links in the main menu. Every library website is a little different, so the link may be phrased in another way or in a different location. But catalogue searches will always be accessible through the homepage.

Once you're on the catalogue page, you should see a drop-down menu that gives you the option to search title keywords, subject area keywords, author names, date of publication, etc. (this may also take the form of several, separate search bars on the page). Generally, you will want to start by searching "title keyword." If that doesn't bring you results that you want, search for "subject keyword" instead.

Start by typing one or two of your keywords into the search bar. If I am researching "Richard Nixon and the Vietnam War in 1968," I wouldn't just type in "Richard Nixon" but would want to include an additional keyword from the topic or my encyclopedia terms (maybe "Richard Nixon Vietnam" or "Richard Nixon 1968" or "Richard Nixon Vietnamization") so that the search returns sources tuned more closely to my subject. You don't want to enter all of your keywords at once, since you might force the search engine to perform a too-narrow search and get back a "0 results" answer!

Once you find a source in the library catalogue that looks interesting (whether it can be downloaded or not) use the information on the source's catalogue page to find other related sources. For example, if I search "Richard Nixon Vietnam," a title keyword search might bring up the book *Richard Nixon and the Vietnam War: The End of the American Century*, along with other books that focus on the period before 1968 and aren't related to my overall topic. However, when I click on the title *Richard Nixon and the Vietnam War: The End of the American Century,* the catalogue page for the source (the page that loads when you click the title) includes a link to the subject area "Vietnam War, 1961-1975—United States." When I click that link, I find even more sources related to my overall paper subject. So you can build a resource list off individual sources, especially if a particular series of keywords doesn't immediately bring up the sources you want. Research takes some trial and error and you may need to play around and swap out your keywords a few times before you find what you want.

Depending on what the search returns and what your library has digitized, you may be able to immediately access the sources you choose online. If not, make a quick list of the titles and call numbers that you want to investigate and check out. Be sure to check the library catalogue page to make sure that the book is on the shelf and hasn't been checked out! Searching titles before you go to the library can save you time and frustration.

If you are really struggling to find sources, you can always contact a reference librarian for help. Reference librarians are trained to search for sources, and can help you navigate the catalogue or other library resources. They can also help you locate your selected sources, or point you towards sections of the library that may have more information on your subject.

Finding online resources

If searching a library catalogue is like maneuvering through a city, something planned and full of easily navigable infrastructure, searching online is like exploring a jungle. If you don't know the overgrown paths, it can be impossible to know whether you are headed in the right direction. But that doesn't mean the search is impossible!

The first thing you need is a guide, a search engine. But if you just type your keywords into Google, you'll come up with all sorts of information from all sorts of sites—some is likely to be good but much of it bad, or at least not what you want. Search engines are software; they search the content of thousands of web pages looking for the key term you have entered. There is no human reading through the sources to vet them or make sure the keyword you typed is being used the same way in the source. Therefore, to make sure you are getting the right information, you need to use search engines that can tailor what they are searching for and are tuned towards mediated sources. So instead of using plain Google, tell the search engine what kinds of sources to search by using news.google.com (news sources), books.google.com (published books), or scholar.google.com (scholarly journals and articles). This will focus the search on specific types of mediated sources, and will automatically get you off to a better start.

Now that you are face to face with your search engine, you need to learn to talk to it!

Software thinks differently than you do. You need to be careful about overwhelming the search with keywords, or not giving it enough detail to find what you need. When entering your key terms into the search engine, be careful not to enter unnecessary words (the, a, an, and, etc.) or punctuation. Punctuation works as a command in search engines, and may alter *how* the engine searches for your keywords. Learning and using common search commands can help you communicate with your search engine efficiently:

Command	What does it do?	Why would I use it?
Quotation Marks ("")	Groups words for finding specific phrases	If you are looking for a full name or a specific phrase, it ensures that the search engine only pulls links for sources that have all of the keywords inside of the quotation marks in the same order. *"Richard Nixon"* will return sources about the president. *Richard Nixon* will tell you about every Richard and every Nixon (including Cynthia!) that the search engine can find.
Addition Sign (+)	Adding a + between key-words means that both keywords on either side of the symbol must be included in the sources pulled by the search engine, but they do not need to be in the same order or even close to one another.	If you need to find information about taxes in Florida, you could type *taxes + Florida* to ensure all sources mention both taxes and Florida. You wouldn't want to use *"Florida taxes"* because it is likely the words won't be in that exact order in every relevant source.
Subtraction Sign (-)	Adding a - between key-words ensures that the search engine seeks the first word, but will eliminate any sources that mention the second word from the search return.	If you are researching the state of Washington, you can type *Washington - D.C.* to ensure none of the sources are focused on Washington D.C. instead of the state.
Asterisk (*)	Can expand a search by searching different endings for a root word	If you want to search food of Mexican origin, but don't know what type, you can search *Mexic* + food*. The search will search for any word with the root "Mexic," including "Mexican," "Mexicali," etc.

Command	What does it do?	Why would I use it?
"Site:"	Allows you to search within a specific site or a specific type of site	If you want to find an article on taxes specifically in *The New York Times,* you can type: *site: nytimes.com taxes* OR If you want to search for a government article on taxes, you can search: *site: .gov taxes.* This will only look for articles on .gov (government run) sites

Much like a library catalogue, specific search engines have advanced search options that you can use to help narrow your search. Once you have the settings to your liking, you can enter your key terms using the appropriate commands. Again, this may take some trial and error, but you should eventually be able to find sources related to your subject.

Keep in mind that in libraries, experts curate the sources available, so all sources in a library have been determined as mediated sources. So for online sources, you will need to check and double check the reliability of the source. Happy hunting!

- You must have a clear topic before you begin researching sources.
- You can determine your search terms by pre-reading about your topic in encyclopedia entries and jotting down any names, places, or ideas related to your subject.
- You can use your decided search terms in the library catalogue and also when researching through online search engines.
- Before you go to a library, search the online catalogue for sources (both digital and print) related to your topic.
- You can use the information on a source's catalogue page to lead you to other sources in the catalogue on similar topics that may not have appeared in your original search.
- You can contact, online or in person, your library's reference or research desk for additional help finding sources or navigating the catalogue.

- Online research is not curated, so it can sometimes take longer to find sources that fit your topic.
- Using search engines with specific focuses (like scholar.google.com, books.google.com, or news.google.com) can help you narrow your search and find more reliable sources.
- Use command punctuation to tell your search engine how to "read" your search terms.
- Searching in library catalogues or online can involve a lot of trial and error—just keep playing with your search terms and search options!

Quick Reference

- Sources provide reliable information that you will use to formulate your ideas and support your claims in a paper.
- Sources can be books, articles, videos, website content, and any other medium that provides information related to your paper topic.
- Mediated sources are sources that have been fact-checked or edited by someone other than the author.
- Unmediated sources are sources that have not been fact-checked by a third party.
- You only want to use mediated sources for your research papers.
- You must have a clear topic before you begin researching sources.
- You can determine your search terms by pre-reading about your topic in encyclopedia entries and jotting down any names, places, or ideas related to your subject.
- You can use your chosen search terms in the library catalogue and also when researching through online search engines.
- Before you go to a library, search the online catalogue for sources (both digital and print) related to your topic.
- You can use the information on a source's catalogue page to lead you to other sources in the catalogue on similar topics that may not have appeared in your original search.

- You can contact, online or in person, your library's reference or research desk for additional help finding sources or navigating the catalogue.
- Online research is not curated, so it can sometimes take longer to find sources that fit your topic.
- Using search engines with specific purposes (like scholar.google.com, books.google.com, or news.google.com) can help you narrow your search and find more reliable sources.
- Use command punctuation to tell your search engine how to "read" your search terms.
- Searching in library catalogues or online can involve a lot of trial and error—just keep playing with your search terms and search options!

Part 2
Taking Notes

What sorts of notes should I take?

Think about sources as your foundation—they provide the necessary information for you to formulate your ideas, arguments, and conclusions on a specific topic. As you read through your sources, you should take notes on any interesting information, facts, or quotes that are relevant to your paper topic. Notes should be short for easy assembly later in the writing process (see Part 5). But even when you keep your notes brief, by the end of the researching and note-taking process, you should have a great deal of raw material. You'll use your notes to construct your draft, putting the information in as quotes, summarized information, and paraphrased ideas. (We'll talk about each of these.)

But before we move on, let's talk about *how* to take notes efficiently.

Before you can begin taking notes, you must have a clear topic that you intend to gather information on. That topic will be your guiding light as you seek information. When taking notes, you must stay focused on one particular thing, and only jot down information related to that idea. If you don't stay focused, you could end up copying out most of the source—which is very time consuming and would lead to an unfocused paper.

For example, while researching Richard Nixon and the Vietnam War, I might encounter this paragraph from Larry Berman's *No Peace, No Honor: Nixon, Kissinger, and Betrayal in Vietnam:*

> Johnson's patience was wearing thin. He did not want to stop all of the bombing of North Vietnam when the communists had not ceased infiltration and were poised for another offensive. On July 26,

1968, he invited Republican candidate Richard Nixon to the White House in order to hear the probable Republican nominee's views on Vietnam. Rusk and Rostow were the only others present. Nixon made it very clear that he did not favor a bombing pause because bombing was "one piece of leverage you have left." As Nixon was leaving the White House, he told LBJ, "I do not intend to advocate for a bombing pause." LBJ was certainly leaning the same way.[1]

Since my paper topic is Nixon and the Vietnam War, I only want to jot down information relevant to my topic and ignore everything else. Here are what my notes would look like:

> Berman, Larry. *No Peace, No Honor: Nixon, Kissinger, and Betrayal in Vietnam.* New York: Free Press, 2001.
>
> Nixon "made it very clear that he did not favor a bombing pause" (27)
> He saw bombings as a crucial political tool (27)

The rest of the information in the paragraph is about Johnson, not Nixon—so I wouldn't write it down.

Remember: take your notes on a very focused topic! You can always return to the source later if you need more.

- Before you can write your paper, you need to take notes by summarizing and quoting information in the source that is relevant to your paper topic.
- Notes should be short for easy organization later on.
- You only want to take note of information relevant to your paper topic.
- That information will serve as the basis for your draft.

---

1. Larry Berman, *No Peace, No Honor: Nixon, Kissinger, and Betrayal in Vietnam* (Free Press, 2001), 27.

How do I keep track of who said what?

Notice how my notes are written in a particular format. When writing notes, you always want to follow four basic rules:

1. Always write down the full source information (author, title, place of publication, publisher, and year of publication) as if you were writing a Works Cited entry (we'll cover this in Part 3, don't worry!). Then, list your notes from that source below. This ensures that you know what source you have found the notes from.

2. You can either quote directly from your source, and use quotation marks around the exact wording from the source (as in my first note), or you can paraphrase the information in your own words (like in my second note). We'll talk more about the difference in a minute. But either way, be sure to follow the next rule:

3. Always write the page number of the source next to the notes so that you know where exactly you found that information.

4. If you are reading an eBook or online source, never copy and paste words into your notes. Always write or type your notes out. This forces your brain to process the information and begin forming connections between ideas and bits of information even before you begin drafting. When you copy and paste, you'll always put *too much information* in your notes—and that will slow you down when you begin writing.

These rules will save you time, as you won't need to go back and find the source information later when you include documentation in your essays. But most importantly, these rules will help you avoid plagiarism. If you always include quotation marks around the exact phrasing you have taken from the source, you are more likely to include those quotation marks again when you begin drafting. By including the source information and page numbers, you also have all the necessary information for writing your footnotes efficiently.

There are two primary ways to take notes: on index cards or in a word-processing program such as Microsoft Word.

Traditionally, students have been taught to take notes on 3x5 index cards, using a different card for each quote. The first card would include the full bibliographical information, while the rest of the cards include just the author's name. But now that many students use word processors more frequently, using index cards isn't necessary. Typing your notes in a word processor document, with the source information at the top and notes listed below, can be a more efficient method. But it can also lead you to take *too many* notes. Always try to distill the information you need down into as few words as possible!

- When you start taking notes, always write down the full source information (author, title, place of publication, publisher, and year of publication) as if you were writing a Works Cited entry. Then list your notes from that source below.
- Your notes should include a mix of direct and indirect (paraphrased) quotes from the source.
- Always include the page number next to the notes so that you know where exactly you found that information.
- When taking notes from online sources, never copy and paste words or phrases into your notes. You should always write (or type) your notes out.
- You can write your notes on index cards (with each note on its own card and the full source information written on the first note card) or in a word processor document.

What's the difference between paraphrasing and quoting?

Notice in the above examples that I use a mix of **quoted** and **paraphrased** information. Quoted information is when the exact words of the author are used in your notes, surrounded by quotation marks (see rule #2 above). Paraphrased information, however, is when you use your own words to explain what the author is saying in the source. When you start taking notes, you will need to decide what information should be quoted and what information should be paraphrased. Deciding this early on can make the drafting process much smoother and help you avoid gathering too much information.

Essentially, you will use quotes to highlight interesting language used by one of your sources, or to give specific details about your topic that can't be found elsewhere. So you only want to quote interesting phrasings about your subject that will help elevate your writing later on. I included the quote that Nixon "made it very clear that he did not favor a bombing pause" because I found the phrasing "bombing pause" to be particularly interesting in how it frames Nixon's beliefs and ideas. If I were to rephrase it to:

Nixon didn't want to stop the bombings

some of the power of the sentence is lost.

Paraphrasing should be used to take note of the "gist" of a sentence or summarize a long passage where the language of the source is not essential. As mentioned above, your notes should stay laser focused on your paper subject. This means that much of the information you encounter in your source will not be necessary for your paper. But if you only wrote down direct quotes, removing them from their context, you might not understand (or remember by the time you start drafting) why the quotes are important (or worse: what they are about). Paraphrasing information can help you summarize the context of a quote without getting bogged down in details that might not be as relevant to your paper.

You can also use paraphrasing to summarize a long passage. Generally, notes should be short (this will be critical when you begin organizing them for your draft, see Part 5), and summary is your main tool in achieving this. Let's say, for example, I came across this paragraph when reading *Richard Nixon and the Vietnam War: The End of the American Century* by David F. Schmitz for my paper on Richard Nixon and the Vietnam War in 1968:

The initial American commitment to Vietnam stemmed from the post-war policy of containment. After World War II, American officials came to see the Soviet Union as a new threat to American interests and world peace. The Truman administration saw Russian policies as inherently aggressive, expansive, and hostile to the West and understood communism as a monolithic force directed by Moscow that threatened to spread to all parts of the world. As such, it constituted another totalitarian threat to freedom, similar to fascism, with which there could be no compromise. The United States again faced an enemy that represented the antithesis of the values and a threat to its security. At Munich, American officials had learned the key lesson of the 1930s: aggression cannot be appeased. From Washington's vantage point, it was a bipolar world, a struggle between freedom and totalitarianism, in which all international events were linked to the battle against communism.

While the information in this paragraph isn't directly related to my paper topic, it does provide some insight into the causes of the Vietnam War that might provide some context to my notes on the war itself and Nixon's policies. So instead of taking notes on all of the details in the paragraph, I can simply paraphrase it in my notes:

Schmitz, David F. *Richard Nixon and the Vietnam War: The End of the American Century*. Lanham, Md.: Rowman & Littlefield, 2014.

America's involvement in Vietnam was part of the U.S.'s larger policy of stopping the spread of communism after WWII (1-2)

Using a mix of quotes and summary is essential for taking good notes that will be easy to bring together later. Think of quotes as the spice of your paper. They are intended to add zip and pizzazz to your sentences by showing interesting support for your ideas or contributing phrasing that shines light on the opinions of experts on the subject. Overuse them and your own ideas will be overpowered—it will look as though you're just assembling other people's ideas. Underuse them, and your paper will be bland and uninteresting. You can strike a balance early on if you are attentive to the balance of quotes and paraphrasing in your notes.

- Notes should include a mix of quoted and paraphrased information.
- Quotes are used to indicate the exact words of the author and should be used to highlight interesting phrasings and opinions from the source.
- Paraphrasing is when you use your words to summarize the meaning of a source.
- Paraphrasing can be used to summarize large chunks of text or to provide context for quotes.
- You don't need an exact balance, but you should be attentive to how many quotes versus summaries you are using as you take notes.

Quick Reference

- Before you can write your paper, you need to take notes by summarizing and quoting information in the source that is relevant to your paper topic.
- Notes should be short for easy organization later on.
- You only want to take note of information relevant to your paper topic.
- That information will serve as the basis for your draft.
- When you start taking notes, always write down the full source information (author, title, place of publication, publisher, and year of publication) as if you were writing a Works Cited entry. Then list your notes from that source below.
- Your notes should include a mix of direct and indirect quotes from the source.
- Always include the page number next to the notes so that you know where exactly you found that information.
- When taking notes from online sources, never copy and paste words or phrases into your notes. You should always write (or type) your notes out.

- You can write your notes on index cards (with each note on its own card and the full source information written on the first note card) or in a word processor document.
- Notes should include a mix of quoted and paraphrased information.
- Quotes are used to indicate the exact words of the author and should be used to highlight interesting phrasings and opinions from the source.
- Paraphrasing is when you use your words to summarize the meaning of a source.
- Paraphrasing can be used to summarize large chunks of text or to provide context for quotes.
- You don't need an exact balance, but you should be attentive to how many quotes versus summaries you are using as you take notes.

Part 3
Documentation

What is documentation?

It's essential to tell your reader where you found the information you use throughout your research paper. After all of the hard work you have put into your research, you don't want your reader thinking that you pulled your information and quotes out of thin air. And what if someone wants to confirm the truth of your facts for themselves?

So how do you show what sources you have used?

If you look carefully at a work of nonfiction, you may notice a few things you wouldn't find in a novel. For example, you might see a sentence followed by a brief superscript number:

> Through the nineteenth century, the role of newspapers and magazines in American life began to shift. According to Richard Ohmann, editors began dropping prices and manipulating the content of newspapers and magazines to appeal to larger audiences. Instead of serving as mouthpieces for political factions and ideological movements, editors started to send reporters out to collect information about the community.[1]

That superscript number will then be repeated either at the bottom of the page, or at the end of the chapter, alongside information about the source in which that information was originally found:

¹ Richard Ohmann, *Selling Culture: Magazines, Markets, and Class at the Turn of the Century* (Verso, 1996), 20.

You may also find, at the end of the book, a list titled "Reference" or "Bibliography" or "Works Cited." Here, the author will list all of the sources used throughout the book.

These are all examples of **documentation**: the ways in which the writer is letting you know where information was found. Documentation goes by many names (citations, references, etc.) but its goal is always to identify and give credit to the sources used in the research and writing of the piece.

Documentation can come in many different forms. What type and style of documentation you use will be dependent on your teacher's preferences or class subject area, but this section will provide a general overview of how to use different types of documentation throughout your paper.

- Documentation is the process through which writers show where they found certain information while researching.
- Documentation is sometimes referred to as "citations" or "references."

What types of documentation can I use?

As you gathered your notes to prepare your paper, you picked out direct quotations, summarized paragraphs, and paraphrased (wrote what the author said in your own words). As you add this information to your essay, you will need to declare to your reader where, in that specific source, you found that specific information. There are three types of documentation you can use for that: **footnotes, endnotes**, and **in-text citations**.

Footnotes and endnotes

Footnotes and endnotes are written in the same way. The only difference is where they are placed in your paper. For both, you start by inserting a superscript number at the end of the sentence you have written with the borrowed information. For example:

According to Richard Ohmann, editors began dropping prices and manipulating the content of newspapers and magazines to appeal to larger audiences.[1]

That superscript number will then lead to the footnote or endnote containing the source information. With a footnote, the source information is placed at the bottom of the page where the sentence is (look at the bottom of this page for my footnote). If it is an endnote, the source information will be placed at the end of the paper, either on the last page (for short papers) or on a separate page (for very long papers).

No matter their placement, the source information will always be written in a certain order based on the style of documentation. There are many different styles of documentation: **Turabian, Chicago Manual of Style, Harvard Style, MLA, and APA**. And each one of these styles of documentation has changed over time. I will explain each style later in this chapter, but to begin I am using Turabian style, a style common to student papers:

[1] Author's name, *Title of Book* (Publisher, Year of Publication), page number.

[1] Sheri Fink, *Five Days at Memorial: Life and Death in a Storm-Ravaged Hospital* (Crown Books, 2013), 17.

If there are two authors, list them like this:

[1] Author's name and second author's name, *Title of Book* (Publisher, Year of Publication), page number.

[1] Mary Ann Shaffer and Annie Barrows, *The Guernsey Literary and Potato Peel Pie Society* (Dial Press, 2008), 35.

---

1. Richard Ohmann, *Selling Culture: Magazines, Markets, and Class at the Turn of the Century* (Verso, 1996), 20.

If your quote or borrowed information comes from more than one page in the book, put a hyphen between page numbers:

[1] Author's name, *Title of Book* (Publisher, Year of Publication), page numbers.

[1] Patricia Marks, *Bicycles, Bangs, and Bloomers: The New Woman in the Popular Press* (University Press of Kentucky, 1990), 40-41.

Sometimes a book has been revised, resulting in a new edition. If the book is a second, third, fourth, etc. edition, put that information between the title and publisher information:

[1] Author's name, *Title of Book,* number of edition (Publisher, Year of Publication), page number.

[1] Peter Hollins, *The Science of Rapid Skill Acquisition,* 2nd ed. (PH Learning Inc., 2019), 15.

All of the source information that you will need for any documentation can be found on the copyright page of a source, usually the second or third page. Once you are on the copyright page, look down until you see "Library of Congress Cataloging-in-Publication Data." There, you will find all of the source information you need. Self-published books often lack this data. For such books, use the abbreviation *self-pub* in place of a publishing company.

If you are using an eBook that does not have page numbers, you should provide the chapter or section number and any additional information provided by the eBook to show location. (Check out the section called "How do I cite something that's not a book or article?" below.)

If you're using a word processor, you can easily insert footnotes and endnotes using the "insert footnotes" command. This command is available in all word processors and is usually located under the "Insert" tab in the toolbar at the top of the page. This command will automatically insert the superscript number at the end of the sentence (where your cursor is) and the bottom of the page (or end of the document if you select "endnotes"). All you need to do is type the source information in! This will make your footnotes/endnotes uniform and automatically move them as you revise your work, avoiding any frustrating formatting battles with your word processor.

In-Text citations

In-text citations, as their name suggests, document the source information in the text of the paper. Instead of including a number or having your reader look in another place for the source, the information you need is included at the end of the sentence in parentheses. Turabian in-text citations include the author's last name, year of publication, and page number:

> According to Richard Ohmann, editors began dropping prices and manipulating the content of newspapers and magazines to appeal to larger audiences (Ohmann 1996, 20).

Notice that the closing parenthesis comes at the end of the sentence, but before the period. You can also see that less source information is included here, so as to not take up too much room in the paper and cause a "roadblock" in the flow of your writing. All other information is included in the **Works Cited page**, which I will explain later this chapter.

This type of citation is often used in scientific writing—historical and literary papers are more likely to use endnotes or footnotes.

- There are three types of documentation you can use within your essay to show where exactly you found something in the source: footnotes, endnotes, or in-text citations.
- Footnotes and endnotes in Turabian style are formatted: [1]Author's name, *Title of Book* (Publisher, Year of Publication), page number
- In-text citations in Turabian style are generally formatted: (Author's last name year, page number)

Why are there so many styles?

While the general rules for footnotes, endnotes, and in-text citations are always the same, the *style* may change.

The style I used in the above section, Turabian, is the style most common for student papers. It is named after Kate Turabian, who was the head secretary for the graduate department at the University of Chicago from 1930 to 1958. It was her job to approve all theses and dissertations submitted to the University of Chicago, and therefore she needed to check that these papers followed the University of Chicago's *Manual of Style*. But this manual was massive and very complicated, so students often struggled to understand how to use it or simply made many mistakes.

So Kate Turabian wrote a simplified version of the manual intended for these students. The style I have been explaining is just a more streamlined version of Chicago Manual of Style citations. It's also based on the most recent edition of *The Chicago Manual of Style*—the 17th edition. Remember that I said styles change over time? If you look at Turabian guidelines based on an earlier edition of the *Chicago Manual*, the instructions might be slightly different. Your paper wouldn't be *incorrect* if you used earlier guidelines, but you should always make sure to check with instructors or teachers to find out what edition *they're* using.

Turabian style is almost always acceptable, but once you start writing papers in higher-level classes, you may find that your teachers require another style of documentation. Here is a brief summary of how each of the most common styles would be formatted in a Works Cited page. Notice how the order of information, capitalization, and punctuation changes from version to version! And remember—these are all based on the most recent guidelines that I checked when I wrote this guide. If you're reading *Who Said What?* in 2030, definitely look for the newest rules for each style!

Turabian:

Ohmann, Richard. *Selling Culture: Magazines, Markets, and Class at the Turn of the Century.* New York: Verso, 1996.

Chicago Manual of Style:

> Ohmann, Richard. *Selling Culture: Magazines, Markets, and Class at the Turn of the Century.* New York: Verso, 1996.

APA (American Psychological Association—often used for science writing):

> Ohmann, R. (1996). *Selling culture: magazines, markets, and class at the turn of the century.* New York, NY: Verso.

Harvard:

> Ohmann, R. (1996) *Selling culture: magazines, markets, and class at the turn of the century.* New York: Verso.

MLA (Modern Language Association—often used for arts and humanities writing):

> Ohmann, Richard. *Selling Culture: Magazines, Markets, and Class at the Turn of the Century.* Verso, 1996.

It is easy to look up the different variations of these styles and their changes from year to year. When you type the name of any of the above citation styles into a search engine, the search is likely to return many web pages offering information on how to format the citations correctly.

However, it is important to always make sure you are looking at the most up-to-date guide, as style guides update frequently. For that reason, it is important to ensure that you are looking at the official website. If I type "Chicago Style Citation" into my Google search bar, the official webpage for *The Chicago Manual of Style* comes up as the second result; the page is located at www.chicagomanualofstyle.org.

But the first result is from a website called www.citationmachine.net. Citation Machine is an "automatic citation generator" that promises to format your information correctly if you type it in. Warning: avoid using automatic citation generators like Citation Machine, Zotero or EasyBib. These automated sites are often out of date, or have difficulty assigning the correct source information to the correct location in the citation.

Though citation generators are incredibly unreliable, they remain very popular among students. So it is likely that your search for the style guide will return many of these citation generator websites. But don't be fooled! Just because they are popular does not mean they are useful.

Instead, look for the official website of your chosen style—or else use a recognized university website. If you have difficulty finding the official style guide, there are a few reference sites that are trustworthy and frequently updated to accommodate any changes:

- Purdue Writing Lab
- RefWorks
- LibGuides

Though documentation can be tedious and sometimes frustrating, it is a necessary part of our research papers. Like an iceberg, our papers are just the visible 10% of effort that results from planning, researching, reading, note-taking, and drafting. Your documentation helps show your reader the other 90% below the surface.

- There are many different styles in which you can write your documentation: Turabian, Chicago Manual of Style, Harvard Style, MLA, and APA.
- The style you use depends on the requirements of your paper or teacher, but can easily be researched online.
- When researching how to write documentation for a particular style, you should use the official style guide website or a reliable platform.
- Avoid citation generators at all cost!

How do I cite something that's not a book?

In the above sections, all of the example sources were books, because citations for books are generally the most straightforward. However, when you are writing a research paper, you will often use a wide variety of sources. The types of sources we use for our papers are also always changing. Forty years ago, you couldn't cite a website. Twenty years ago, you couldn't cite an eBook. Ten years ago, you couldn't cite an Instagram post. But now, all of these types of sources can be used and therefore documented in our research papers. Here are rules for how to write footnotes/endnotes for different types of sources in Turabian:

Articles

1. Magazine and newspaper articles

    [1]Author name, "Name of Article," *Name of Magazine/Newspaper*, Date of publication, page number.

    [1]Jaqueline Harp, "A Breed for Every Yard: Black Welsh Mountain Sheep Break New Ground," *Sheep!,* September/October 2013, 27.

2. Academic journal articles

    [1]Author name, "Name of Article," *Title of Journal* volume number, issue number (Date of Publication): page number, DOI

    NOTE: The DOI (or Digital Object Identifier) will only be included with online journal articles and not print ones. This is a URL that is permanently tied to the online publication for easy identification. If the DOI is not provided, you should write the name of the database in which the article was found.

    [1] Ashley Hope Pérez, "Material Morality and the Logic of Degrees in Diderot's *Le neveu de Rameau*," *Modern Philology* 114, no. 4 (May 2017): 874, https://doi.org/10.1086/689836.

    [2] Jean-Christophe Agnew, "Capitalism, Culture and Catastrophe: Lawrence Levine and the Opening of Cultural History,"

The Journal of American History 93, no.3 (December 2006): 774, JSTOR.

Web pages and other digital resources

1. Website content

   [1] Author/editor/sponsoring organization or website, "Name of Article," URL (date accessed).

   [1] Mallory Daugherty, "Baa Baa Black and White Sheep Treats," http://www.southernliving.com/home-garden/holidays-occasions/spring-table-settings-centerpieces-00400000041389/page8.html (accessed Sept. 12, 2013).

2. eBooks with flowing text (meaning: no traditional page numbers)

   [1] Author name, *Name of Book* (Publisher, date of publication), Name of eBook format: Chapter number, and other information given by the eBook platform.

   [1] Paul de Kruif, *Microbe Hunters* (Harvest, 1996), Kindle: Ch. 7, Loc. 2134.

Recordings

1. Films, videos, or other recordings

   [1] Name of creator, "Title of work," name of interviewer or director, Sponsoring organization/distributer, Date of creation or publication, medium, time. URL

   [1] Terisa Folaron, "Comma story," *TEDed,* July 9, 2013, video, 4:59. https://ed.ted.com/lessons/comma-story-terisa-folaron

Social media citations

1. Instagram, Facebook, Twitter, etc.

[1] Name of author/editor/sponsoring organization (handle or user-name if different), "Caption of post," Social media platform and medium, Date of post, URL.

[1] Pete Souza (@petesouza), "Three amigos: President Obama with President of Mexico and Prime Minister of Canada in 2016," Instagram photo, August 28, 2018, https://www.instagram.com/p/BnCWsiCFruM/.

Because the sources available for research are always expanding, you may need to do some research of your own to find out how to cite different types of sources in the future. You can use the steps I outline in the final part of this section for how to research updates in citation style.

- How you format your documentations will change depending on the type of source and will not always look exactly the same.
- You can use a style guide to search how to format your documentation based on the specific types of sources.

How do I make a Works Cited page?

A Works Cited page is a separate page at the end of your paper that lists, in alphabetical order by last name of author, the sources that you have already footnoted. Works Cited pages are always included alongside your in-essay documentation, but are especially important with in-text citations because they include so little source information. But no matter whether you are using footnotes, endnotes, or in-text citations in your paper, you must finalize your paper with a Works Cited page. The Works Cited page will look like this:

Works Cited

Ohmann, Richard. *Selling Culture: Magazines, Markets, and Class at the Turn of the Century.* New York: Verso, 1996.

Works Cited page entries in Turabian style will typically follow the following format:

> Author's last name, first name. *Title of Book.* Place of Publication: Publisher, Date of Publication.

You'll see that while this looks similar to how you write a footnote or endnote, there are some differences. There is no superscript number and all lines other than the first are indented. The citation begins with the last name of the author because your Works Cited page lists your sources alphabetically by author's last name. Look at the following example in Turabian style:

Works Cited

Lutes, Jean Marie. *Front Page Girls: Women Journalists in American Culture and Fiction, 1880-1930.* Ithaca, NY: Cornell University Press, 2006.

Marks, Patricia. *Bicycles, Bangs, and Bloomers: The New Woman in the Popular Press.* Lexington, KY: University Press of Kentucky, 1990.

Ohmann, Richard. *Selling Culture: Magazines, Markets, and Class at the Turn of the Century.* New York: Verso, 1996.

Woods, Marianne Berger. *The New Woman in Print and Pictures: An Annotated Bibliography.* Jefferson, NC: McFarland & Company, Inc., Publishers, 2009.

Notice how Ohmann comes in between Marks and Woods alphabetically. If your reader quickly needs to find information about a source you use, or suddenly thinks, "I wonder where that quote from Richard Ohmann is from," then the reader can quickly go to the Works Cited page and find all of the source information.

You'll also notice that a Works Cited entry provides a little more information about the publisher: the city of publication. This may seem like a random piece of information to add, but this detail can help differentiate publishers in different states or countries with the same names. Since the goal of a Works Cited page is to give your reader a reference list of your sources that they can use to locate the source, knowing the correct publisher is important. If the publisher is located in a well-known city like London, New York, or Los Angeles, you can just include the city name. But if the city is small, or not as well known, you will also want to include the state's abbreviation:

> Bauer, Susan Wise. *Writing with Skill, Level 1.* Charles City, VA: Well-Trained Mind Press, 2012.

When writing a citation, you can simply use the postal code abbreviation of the state name: VA for Virginia. But in some older editions of style manuals, you'll see a pre-postal code used instead. (The state abbreviations now used by the U. S. postal service were first published in 1963—before that, states had a whole different set of abbreviations.) The chart below shows you the difference. All of the two-letter codes are now standard for citations.

Ala.	AL	Alaska	AK	Ariz.	AZ	Ark.	AR	Calif.	CA	Colo.	CO
Conn.	CT	Del.	DE	Fla.	FL	Ga.	GA	Hawaii	HI	Idaho	ID
Ill.	IL	Ind.	IN	Iowa	IA	Kan.	KS	Ky.	KY	La.	LA
Maine	ME	Md.	MD	Mass.	MA	Mich.	MI	Minn.	MN	Miss.	MS
Mo.	MO	Mont.	MT	Neb.	NE	Nev.	NV	N.H.	NH	N.J.	NJ
N.M.	NM	N.Y.	NY	N.C.	NC	N.D.	ND	Ohio	OH	Okla.	OK
Ore.	OR	Pa.	PA	R.I.	RI	S.C.	SC	S.D.	SD	Tenn.	TN
Texas	TX	Utah	UT	Vt.	VT	Va.	VA	Wash.	WA	W.Va.	WV
Wis.	WI	Wyo.	WY	P.R.	PR						

Are there a lot of rules when it comes to Works Cited pages? Yes. Do you need to follow them? Absolutely. So if you cannot find the state or city on the copyright page with the rest of the source information, you can use WorldCat, the largest online library reference tool.

To use it, just go to worldcat.org. Type in the title of the book and the author's last name in the search box and hit "Search." For example, if I needed to find the place of publication for Richard Ohmann's book, I would type "*Selling Culture: Magazines, Markets, and Class at the Turn of the Century*" into the WorldCat search bar and click Search. (I use the quotation marks to tell the search engine that I want that exact title, not all the titles that include those words.) The first result that comes up is the cover of the book along with all of the information that I need, including that Verso is a London publisher.

If something you need isn't immediately available on the search page, click the title of the source to see more detailed information.

Like footnotes and endnotes, entries for Works Cited pages will change depending on the style of documentation and types of sources you are using. Here are some examples of how Works Cited entries are formatted in Turabian for different types of sources:

1. Magazine or newspaper article

    Author last name, first name. "Name of article." *Name of magazine/newspaper* volume number: issue number (Date of publication), range of pages article takes up in magazine.

    Harp, Jacqueline. "A Breed for Every Yard: Black Welsh Mountain Sheep Break New Ground." *Sheep!* 34:5 (September/October 2013), 26-28.

2. Academic journal articles

    Author last name, first name. "Name of article." *Title of Journal* volume number, issue number (Date of Publication): page numbers that the article spans. DOI.

    Pérez, Ashley Hope. "Material Morality and the Logic of Degrees in Diderot's *Le neveu de Rameau*." *Modern Philology* 114, no. 4 (May 2017): 872–98. https://doi.org/10.1086/689836.

Agnew, Jean-Christophe. "Capitalism, Culture and Catastrophe: Lawrence Levine and the Opening of Cultural History." *The Journal of American History* 93, no.3 (December 2006): 772-791. JSTOR.

3. Website content

Author/editor/sponsoring organization of website. "Name of article." URL (date accessed).

Daugherty, Mallory. "Baa Baa Black and White Sheep Treats." http://www. southernliving.com/home-garden/holidays-occasions /spring-table-settings-centerpieces-00400000041389/page8. html (accessed Sept. 12, 2013).

4. Ebooks with flowing text (meaning no page numbers)

Author last name, first name. *Title of Book.* City of Publication: Publisher, Date of publication. Name of Ebook format.

De Kruif, Paul. *Microbe Hunters*. Eugene, Ore.: Harvest, 1996. Kindle.

5. Films, videos, or other recordings

Name of creator. "Title of work." Name of interviewer or director. Sponsoring organization/distributor, Date of creation or publication. Medium, length of time. URL.

Folaron, Terisa. "Comma story." *TEDEd,* July 9, 2013. video, 4:59. https://ed.ted.com/lessons/comma-story-terisa-folaron.

NOTE: The name of director or interviewer or the sponsoring organization may not be available depending on the type of video or film, so you may not need to include that information.

6. Social media content

> Name of author/editor/sponsoring organization (handle or user-
> name if different). "Caption of post." Social media platform,
> Date of post. URL.

> Pete Souza (@petesouza). "Three amigos: President Obama with
> President of Mexico and Prime Minister of Canada in 2016."
> Instagram photo, August 28, 2018. https://www.instagram.
> com/p/BnCWsiCFruM/.

These examples provide a general guide for how different source entries
might be formatted in a Works Cited page. But like other types of documentation, the formats are regularly updated, so it is important to check style guides
for the most up-to-date versions.

- Works Cited pages are always included alongside other forms of documentation and provide a complete list at the end of the paper, alphabetized by author's last name, of all the sources documented in the paper.
- Works Cited entries for books in Turabian style are formatted: Author's
  last name, first name. *Title of Book*. Place of Publication: Publisher,
  Year of Publication. p. #. The second line of the entry will typically be
  indented.
- Information used for documentation can usually be found on the copyright page of a book, but WorldCat can help you find any information
  not on that page.
- Like footnotes/endnotes, the Works Cited entry will change depending
  on the style and type of source, so you should be sure to look up the
  most current formatting on the appropriate style guide.

Quick Reference

- Documentation is the process through which writers show where they
  found certain information while researching.
- Documentation is sometimes referred to as "citations" or "references."

- There are three types of documentation you can use within your essay to show where exactly you found something in the source: footnotes, endnotes, or in-text citations.
- Footnotes and endnotes in Turabian style are formatted: [1] Author's name, *Title of Book* (Publisher, Year of Publication), p. #.
- In-text citations in Turabian style are generally formatted: (author's last name year, p. #).
- There are many different styles in which you can write your documentation: Turabian, Chicago Manual of Style, Harvard Style, MLA, and APA.
- The style you use depends on the requirements of your paper or teacher, but can easily be researched online.
- When researching how to write documentation for a type of source or particular style, you should use the official style guide website or a reliable platform.
- Avoid citation generators at all cost!
- How you format your documentation will change depending on the type of source and will not always look exactly the same.
- You can use a style guide to search how to format your documentation based on the specific types of sources.
- Works Cited pages are always included alongside other forms of documentation and provide a complete list at the end of the paper, alphabetized by author's last name, of all the sources documented in the paper.
- Works Cited entries for books in Turabian style are formatted: Author's last name, first name. *Title of Book*. Place of Publication: Publisher, Year of Publication. p. #. The second line of the entry will typically be indented.
- Information used for documentation can usually be found on the copyright page of a book, but WorldCat can help you find any information not on that page.
- Like footnotes/endnotes, the Works Cited entry will change depending on the style and type of source, so you should be sure to look up the most current formatting on the appropriate style guide.

Part 4
How to Avoid Stealing

Why do we document our sources?

Documentation is complicated! Many of the rules may seem silly, and you may wonder why there are so many small things that you need to check and double check to make sure your documentation is written correctly.

So you may be asking yourself: WHAT'S THE POINT?

One goal of writing documentation correctly is for your reader to be able to find the exact same information or quote you have used in your paper. The specific details of your footnotes, endnotes, or in-text citations are intended to point your reader to an exact location in a source. Theoretically, your reader could fact-check you, but more often a curious reader might simply want to read more on the subject.

But for the purposes of this book and your writing classes, you need to document for a much simpler reason: So that you avoid unintentional **plagiarism**.

- Documentation should show your reader exactly where you found a quote or piece of information from a source.
- Documentation is the system through which we give proper credit.

What is plagiarism?

If you use someone else's words or ideas without giving them credit, you are plagiarizing. Even well-known authors are sometimes caught using ideas and sentences that aren't their own! It is vitally important that you avoid this trap.

Plagiarizing words

You should not use someone else's exact words without giving them credit. Include accurately written documentation for all borrowed quotes from any source, and surround any borrowed words or phrases in quotation marks. Since you are explicitly using someone else's phrasing, it only makes sense that you should give credit.

Imagine that you were collecting information to write an essay on Charles I of England, and came across the following passage:

> The executioner, who wore a mask that he might not be known, began to adjust the hair of the prisoner by putting it up under his cap. When the king, supposing that he was going to strike, hastily told him to wait for the sign, the executioner said that he would. The king spent a few minutes on prayer, and then stretched out his hands, which was the sign which he had arranged to give. The axe descended.

If you used this information in your own essay, you would not want to write:

> Charles I ascended the scaffold for his execution. He spent a few minutes in prayer, and then stretched out his hands. The executioner swung the axe and beheaded him.

If you did that, the second sentence in your paragraph would use the exact same words ("spent a few minutes on prayer, and then stretched out his hands") as the third sentence in the original paragraph—with only one change, using *in* instead of *on*. All the rest of the words are the same. Using the author's words without acknowledging him or her is the most obvious form of plagiarism! Instead, you would want to surround the author's words in quotation marks and write:

> Charles I ascended the scaffold for his execution. He "spent a few minutes on prayer, and then stretched out his hands."[1] The executioner swung the axe and beheaded him.

> [1] Jacob Abbott, *History of King Charles the First of England* (Henry Altemus Company, 1900), 282.

To avoid plagiarism, put quotation marks around any words taken directly from another source, and also provide documentation (like the footnote in the example above).

Plagiarizing ideas

Plagiarism can occur even if you aren't using an exact quote—even if you move the words around or change them completely. Even if you paraphrase what a source says, using your own words, you're still using someone else's ideas. So you always need to use documentation to show where you find your ideas. That means that you also need to include documentation for any sentence, even if it doesn't include a quote, that includes borrowed information.

In 2006, a major publisher published a novel called *How Opal Mehta Got Kissed, Got Wild, and Got a Life.* The novel was written by a freshman college student named Kaavya Viswanathan. She received a lot of attention for writing the book at such a young age. But readers soon pointed out that some of the ideas, scenes, and descriptions were very, very close to ideas and scenes in novels by four other writers. Look through the following chart to see the similarities:

Viswanathan's Book	Other Books
"He had too-long shaggy brown hair that fell into his eyes, which were always half shut. His mouth was always curled into a half smile, like he knew about some big joke that was about to be played on you." (p. 48)	"He's got dusty reddish dreads that a girl could never run her hands through. His eyes are always half-shut. His lips are usually curled in a semi smile, like he's in on a big joke that's being played on you but you don't know it yet." (Megan McCafferty, *Sloppy Firsts* [Random House, 2001], p. 23)
"Five department stores, and 170 specialty shops later, I was sick of listening to her hum along to Alicia Keys . . ." (p. 51)	"Finally, four major department stores and 170 specialty shops later, we were done." (McCafferty, p. 237)
"Poster reads, 'If from drink you get your thrill, take precaution—write your will.' " (p. 118)	"Warning reads, 'If from speed you get your thrill / take precaution—make your will.' " (Salman Rushdie, *Haroun and the Sea of Stories* [Granta Books, 1991], p. 35)
"And I'll tell everyone that in eighth grade you used to wear a 'My Little Pony' sweatshirt to school every day," I continued. Priscilla gasped. "I didn't!" she said, her face purpling again. "You did! I even have pictures," I said. "And I'll make it public that you named your dog Pythagoras . . ." Priscilla opened her mouth and gave a few soundless gulps . . . "Okay, fine!" she said in complete consternation. "Fine! I promise I'll do whatever you want. I'll talk to the club manager. Just please don't mention the sweatshirt. Please." (p. 282)	"And we'll tell everyone you got your Donna Karan coat from a discount warehouse shop." Jemima gasps. "I didn't!" she says, colour suffusing her cheeks. "You did! I saw the carrier bag," I chime in. "And we'll make it public that your pearls are cultured, not real . . ." Jemima claps a hand over her mouth . . . "OK!" says Jemima, practically in tears. "OK! I promise I'll forget all about it. I promise! Just please don't mention the discount warehouse shop. Please." (Sophie Kinsella, *Can You Keep a Secret?* [Random House, 2005], p. 350)

"The whole time, Frederic (I wondered if anyone dared call him Freddie) kept picking up long strands of my hair and making sad faces. 'It must go,' he said. 'It must all go.' And it went. Not all of it, because after four inches vanished, I started making panicked, whimpering sounds that touched even Frederic's heart . . ." (p. 57)	"Meanwhile, Paulo was picking up chunks of my hair and making this face and going, all sadly, 'It must go. It must all go.' And it went. All of it. Well, almost all of it. I still have some like bangs and a little fringe in back." (Meg Cabot, *The Princess Diaries* [HarperCollins, 2001], p. 128)
"Every inch of me had been cut, filed, steamed, exfoliated, polished, painted, or moisturized. I didn't look a thing like Opal Mehta. Opal Mehta didn't own five pairs of shoes so expensive they could have been traded in for a small sailboat. She didn't wear makeup or Manolo Blahniks or Chanel sunglasses or Habitual jeans. . . . She never owned enough cashmere to make her concerned for the future of the Kazakhstani mountain goat population. I was turning into someone else." (p. 59)	"There isn't a single inch of me that hasn't been pinched, cut, filed, painted, sloughed, blown dry, or moisturized. . . . Because I don't look a thing like Mia Thermopolis. Mia Thermopolis never had fingernails. Mia Thermopolis never had blond highlights. Mia Thermopolis never wore makeup or Gucci shoes or Chanel skirts. . . . I don't even know who I am anymore. It certainly isn't Mia Thermopolis. She's turning me into someone else." (Cabot, p. 12)

When my students see this example, sometimes they start to panic: "What if I accidently say something similar to what has been in another book? Will I be plagiarizing even if I had never seen it before? Even if it was an accident?" No, of course not. Millions of gallons of ink have been spilt since humans started writing, and it is likely that you will at some point write something identical to what someone has written or said before without even realizing it. If just *one* of the above similarities had been in Viswanathan's book, it could have been a coincidence. But because there were so many details and scenes borrowed from the same four writers (these are just a few of the many similarities!), it seemed clear that this was plagiarism.

Plagiarizing images

Plagiarism doesn't just apply to writing either. In the fashion industry, copying designs is often a source of industry scandal. Companies like Zara and Urban Outfitters frequently come under fire for mimicking designs of small-scale boutiques that post images of their goods on Etsy. Recently, Urban Outfitters was accused of stealing a graphic design from an artist's Tumblr to use as a skirt print. The artist's design, marketed under the name *Spires*, was an art print—a poster. The Urban Outfitters design was identical—but printed on a skirt.

While the use of the design is different than the context of the artist's original intention, Urban Outfitters is still stealing the artist's intellectual property, because they are using the artist's design to make a profit. The skirt was eventually removed from the Urban Outfitters website, but only after the artist publicly accused the clothing company of stealing his idea.

The international clothing brand Zara has been accused by over forty artists of stealing their designs. Tuesday Bassen, an artist in Los Angeles, posted images on Instagram that compare her pin and patches designs with Zara's alleged rip-off versions. Her post inspired many other artists to bring up claims against Zara. One artist, Adam Kurtz, has even created a website called "Shop Art Theft" which offers side by side comparisons of independent artists' designs and the Zara rip-offs. The website provides links on where to buy the originals, with the hope of supporting the original artists. But this site also makes clear the large scope of Zara's plagiarism.

If you're interested, I encourage you to do a web search for "Urban Outfitters" "plagiarism" and "Zara" to find out more! All of these examples show us that plagiarism happens not only when we borrow words, but also when we borrow ideas or concepts. So even if you are borrowing an idea rather than a direct quote, it is still important that you give the original source credit.

Let's return to our original example about Charles I. Another way of writing the paragraph on the execution might be:

> Charles I ascended the scaffold for his execution. He prayed for a few moments, and then he extended his hands in a sign.[1] The executioner swung the axe and beheaded him.

[1] Jacob Abbott, *History of King Charles the First of England* (Henry Altemus Company, 1900), 282.

In this version, the words have been changed from the original essay by Abbott. But because the idea of Charles's praying and then stretching out his hands comes directly from Abbott's book, it still needs to be documented.

- Borrowing words and ideas without giving proper credit is plagiarism.
- You must always include documentation alongside any quoted material.
- All quoted material must also be surrounded in quotation marks.
- Even if you rephrase authors' ideas in your own words, you must still include documentation because their ideas are their intellectual property.
- Always include documentation for all borrowed information: quotes, ideas, and images.

What is common knowledge?

Now, you might be saying to yourself: "If I am doing a research paper, isn't all of the information borrowed? Do I just cite every single sentence I write?"

Not necessarily! You are not required to cite information that is **common knowledge**. Common knowledge is anything that is widely known by a large group of people—as opposed to something that can only be found in limited sources. You do not need to include documentation for common knowledge because it cannot be attributed to a single source. Any common knowledge you use in your essays, even if it is information you found in a source (or many of your sources), does not need documentation.

Generally, the following are considered common knowledge:

Historical dates	"World War I ended on the 11th of November 1918." "On July 4, 1776, the Declaration of Independence was signed."
Historical facts	"World War I began with the assassination of Archduke Franz Ferdinand." "The American Revolution ended British colonial rule over the thirteen colonies."
Widely accepted scientific facts	"Earthquakes are caused by shifting tectonic plates." "Clouds can easily be explained as water vapor and small water droplets in the Earth's atmosphere."
Geographical facts	"The state of Virginia sits between North Carolina to the south and Maryland to the north." "The Pacific Ocean touches both Japan and California."
Genealogical facts	"John Quincy Adams was former president John Adams' son." "Queen Elizabeth II is married to Prince Philip."
Definitions	"Snow is frozen and condensed water in the atmosphere." "Mammals are warm blooded and give birth to live young."
Proverbs and sayings	"The early bird catches the worm." "They were like two peas in a pod."
Well-known theories or ideas	"Objects are pulled to the Earth by gravity." "Light cannot escape a black hole."
Anything that can be observed with your senses	"Hurricanes bring strong winds that can topple trees and send large debris flying." "The Arctic Circle is covered in a sheet of ice."

From my experience teaching essay writing, common knowledge can be one of the most difficult concepts for students to fully grasp. Here are some common questions that students ask about common knowledge and my answers:

1. *What if I didn't know a piece of information before reading it in a source— is it still common knowledge?*

   Even if you haven't encountered the information before, if it falls under one of the above categories, it still counts as common knowledge. Common knowledge is commonly known by sources and the general public.

2. *What if my sentence has both common knowledge and borrowed information like a quote? Do I need a citation?*

   Yes. If your sentence mixes common knowledge and a quote, you should include a citation for the quote. But you do not need to worry about citing the information considered common knowledge.

3. *What if I can't tell the difference between common knowledge and borrowed information?*

   When in doubt, include a citation. The worst thing that could happen: You have a lot of footnotes (and that is generally considered better than plagiarism).

Let's look at an example of how common knowledge and borrowed information work together in a paper. Read through the following passage from *The History of the Renaissance World*, by Susan Wise Bauer. It describes the invasion of Jurchen tribes in the north of the Chinese empire ruled by the Song dynasty:

> The emperor Song Gaozong, who had just turned twenty when Kaifeng fell, was forced to move from hiding place to hiding place. He grew so desperate that he sent an embassy to the Jurchen generals, offering to become their vassal if the raids would only stop: "I have no one to defend me," he wrote, "and no place to run."[1]

But the Jurchen did not want vassals. The Song scorn was not entirely undeserved; the Jurchen were mounted soldiers with no experience of running a state, no mechanism for administering a conquered country. They wanted to conquer China, not run it as an occupied land.

So Song Gaozong's plea was rejected, and the battles continued. But this turned out to be the saving of the Song. As fighting dragged on, the northern warriors struggled with unfamiliar southern heat. The terrain, crosshatched with streams and canals, slowed their horses. They had no experience with water warfare, but they now faced the barrier of the Yangtze. The Jurchen troops, growing fatter with plunder and loot, were less inclined to ride hard and far. And the Song themselves, adjusting to their exile, were mounting an increasingly powerful resistance by ship.[2]

[1] Yuan-Kang Wang, *Harmony and War: Confucian Culture and Chinese Power Politics* (Columbia University Press, 2001), 80.

[2] Peter Allan Lorge, *War, Politics and Society in Early Modern China, 900–1795* (Routledge, 2005), 55.

The first footnote is used because of the quotes: anytime you borrow an author's words, you must include a footnote (or any form of documentation). But there are no quotes in the third paragraph, so why is there a footnote at the very end?

As the writer was researching the Jurchen invasion, she found that many historians describe the Jurchen invasion of southern China. The fact that it occurred is something we can consider common knowledge, because it is a historical fact commonly found in all (or most) of the sources the writer consulted. However, the explanation for why the invasion failed is specific to a particular source, because one historian theorized a specific explanation for the failure. The historian's theory and ideas, even though the writer put them in her own words, still originated with one author and deserve credit.

However, the second paragraph has no documentation. That is because the statement that the Jurchen were mounted soldiers who were not used to governing is a fact that anyone could conclude by looking at the Jurchen's history. Therefore, this information is common knowledge and does not need to be documented.

In the second paragraph, the writer also comes to the conclusions that the Jurchen did not want vassals and "wanted to conquer China, not run it as an occupied land." These are ideas that the writer formulated herself after having read many histories on the Jurchen. If someone were to read this source and use that opinion, they would need to cite the author of this excerpt in their own writing.

To sum up: if you come to your own opinion about something, you do not need to cite it. However, if you borrow an author's conclusion, opinion, or ideas on a topic, you need to give that writer credit because it is that writer's intellectual property.

- You do not need to document common knowledge, because it is information that is widely known and not specific to a source.
- Common knowledge includes facts (historical facts, dates, genealogical facts, geographical facts) and widely agreed upon ideas (sayings and proverbs, definitions, well-known theories, anything observed through the senses).
- Even if it is something you didn't know before (like a date), it can still count as common knowledge because it is commonly known throughout sources.
- You do not need to cite your own conclusions on a topic.
- If you borrow an author's conclusions or opinions on a topic in a paper, you do need to provide documentation.

What are the real-world consequences of plagiarism?

The rule against plagiarism isn't just a classroom idea, meant to keep people from cheating on their term papers. It is part of an important system put into place to protect people's intellectual property (meaning their original words or ideas), from being copied and stolen. A good example of this is Fareed Zakaria, who at the time was a journalist for *CNN, Time,* and *The Washington Post.* In 2012, he was found to have plagiarized a column on gun control by copying language from an article written by the historian Jill Lepore on the same subject. Look at their language side by side:

Fareed Zakaria	Jill Lepore
"Laws that banned the carrying of concealed weapons were passed in Kentucky and Louisiana in 1813. Other states soon followed. … Similar laws were passed in Texas, Florida, and Oklahoma. As the governor of Texas (Texas!) explained in 1893, the 'mission of the concealed deadly weapon is murder.'"	"Laws banning the carrying of concealed weapons were passed in Kentucky and Louisiana in 1813, and other states soon followed. … Similar laws were passed in Texas, Florida, and Oklahoma. As the governor of Texas explained in 1893, the 'mission of the concealed deadly weapon is murder.'"

You can see that the phrasing is almost identical. Zakaria admitted to plagiarism not long after he was accused.

His television show on *CNN* was suspended—but eventually returned to regular airings. Though this seems like a minor consequence, it is an act that permanently affects his credibility as a journalist. Zakaria could have avoided this public embarrassment and the effect on his career—if he had simply attributed the sentences to Lepore and given her credit.

Interested in reading more examples of plagiarism in the world around you? Use an internet search engine and read at least two articles about each of the following public figures. Be sure to surround their name in quotation marks and add the word *plagiarism* to your search entry. Refer back to Part 1 if you need a refresher on online research.

1. Chris Spence
2. Margaret Wente
3. Jonah Lehrer
4. Stephen Ambrose

5. Doris Kearns Goodwin
6. Chris Anderson
7. Lance Hindt

When finished reading, either [1] write one or two sentences explaining or [2] verbally discuss with a family member or friend what each person did and why they were accused of plagiarism. Doing this last part will ensure that you understand each unique situation and will help you wrap your brain around the complexities of each issue!

- Avoiding plagiarism is not just a classroom policy to help avoid cheating—it has real world effects!

What's the deal with copyright?

In the last chapter, I mentioned finding all of the information you need for your footnotes or endnotes on the copyright page of a book. But that was the one and only time I mentioned copyright when it comes to documentation. You've probably heard of **copyright** before: either you've seen a "©" at the end of a name or you've heard of some copyright scandal in the news. But rarely do students get a full explanation of what exactly copyright is.

Copyright is essentially a legal right that gives the author of an original work the rights to determine where and when their work is used or copied by others. In the United States, there are several laws that work together to determine who owns a piece of work and when. For example, under U.S. copyright law, anything published before 1923 is no longer protected by copyright law and exists within the public domain. This means that old poems or stories can be copied or re-printed publicly without anyone having to ask the original author or owner of the copyright for permission.

You would still have to cite and document if you quoted from these pre-1923 works! Just because something is out of copyright doesn't mean that you can steal it and pretend that those are your own words! Copyright doesn't have anything to do with documentation—it has to do with *how much* of a source you can directly quote in your own work without asking for permission, and probably paying a fee, to quote it.

When writing research papers for an academic class or project, you won't need to worry about copyright laws as long as you are appropriately document-ing your sources. Because this book intends to explain avoiding plagiarism in student research papers, I will not go into further detail about copyright law since it doesn't apply to student papers. However, if you do write a paper that you intend to publish, either for profit or public consumption, you will likely need to investigate copyright laws further to make sure that your work abides by copyright law.

Copyright laws may seem complex and daunting, but there are many resources available to help students (and even experienced writers) navigate the laws. I suggest *Copyright Law in a Nutshell* by Mary LaFrance, which is short, easy to read, and has a very detailed table of contents for quick reference. I use the third edition in this book, but it is constantly being updated to accom-modate new laws.

- Copyright laws vary by country, but ultimately give the author of the original work the right to determine when and where their work can be reproduced or used by others.
- Copyright laws do not apply for student papers.
- But if you want to publish something for money or in a widely read publication, you need to make sure your work abides by copyright law.

Quick Reference

- Documentation should show your reader exactly where you found a quote or piece of information from a source.
- Documentation is the system through which we give proper credit.
- Borrowing words and ideas without giving proper credit is plagiarism.
- You must always include documentation alongside any quoted material.
- All quoted material must also be surrounded in quotation marks.

- Even if you rephrase authors' ideas in your own words, you must still include documentation because their ideas are their intellectual property.
- Always include documentation for all borrowed information: quotes, ideas, and images.
- You do not need to document common knowledge, because it is information that is widely known and not specific to a source.
- Common knowledge includes facts (historical facts, dates, genealogical facts, geographical facts) and widely agreed upon ideas (sayings and proverbs, definitions, well-known theories, anything observed through the senses).
- Even if it is something you didn't know before (like a date), it can still count as common knowledge because it is commonly known throughout sources.
- You do not need to cite your own conclusions on a topic.
- If you borrow an author's conclusions or opinions on a topic in a paper, you do need to provide documentation.
- Copyright laws vary by country, but ultimately give the author of the original work the right to determine when and where their work can be reproduced or used by others.
- Avoiding plagiarism is not just a classroom policy to help avoid cheating—it has real world effects!
- Copyright laws do not apply for student papers.
- But if you want to publish something for money or in a widely read publication, you need to make sure your work abides by copyright law.

Part 5
Bringing It All Together

At this point, you have learned how to find reliable sources, take notes, document your sources, and avoid plagiarism in your research papers.

But between taking your notes and documenting your sources, there is (of course!) the messy business of actually writing the paper.

The entire process of drafting and editing your composition falls somewhat outside of the scope of this handbook (and within the scope of your writing program), but let's look at one specific part of it: how to prepare and use your notes in your paper.

How do I use my notes to outline a first draft?

Before you can begin drafting your paper, it is *essential* that you organize your notes to create a roadmap for your paper. You might think, "But I've been reading all of these sources and taking notes for so long! Can't I start writing already?!" Sure. But if you start writing before you organize your notes in a logical way, your draft will likely read as jumbled, or the final flow of thought through your paper will be disconnected. Then you'll spend much more time writing and re-writing your paper than if you had spent the extra time organizing your notes. I always tell my students: organizing should be the hard part, and it will make drafting the easy part.

How you organize your notes will of course depend on the content and requirements for your paper. But an **outline** is an excellent organizational tool that can be applied to almost every type of paper because it allows you to group your notes by topic and organize those groupings in a linear fashion. No matter how complex the paper topic, your explanation or argument must flow from Point A to Point B, and an outline helps you plan each step you'll take between points.

A standard outline for a paper will typically include two **levels**. The first level of an outline, usually marked with a Roman numeral, identifies the main topic or idea of a section. The second level, indicated by capital letters, includes the notes related to the topic indicated by the first level. Here is an example skeleton to help you visualize this:

I. Main idea/point 1
    A. Note related to main point 1
    B. Note related to main point 1
II. Main idea/point 2
    A. Note related to main point 2
    B. Note related to main point 2
    C. Note related to main point 2
    D. Note related to main point 2
III. Main idea/point 3
    A. Note related to main point 3
    B. Note related to main point 3

If you are writing a very long or detailed paper, you may find that you need a third level (noted with numbers) to help you organize your information. In that case, the second level can be used to classify subtopics of the main topic:

I. Main idea/point 1
    A. Subtopic for main point 1
        1. note related to subtopic
        2. note related to subtopic
    B. Subtopic for main point 1
        1. note related to subtopic
        2. note related to subtopic

Now that you can see the structure of an outline, you might be wondering how you fit your own notes into such a mold. This is challenging and highly dependent on the topic and requirements of your paper. However, there are some general steps you can take to organize your notes into an outline.

Let's say I've written the following notes for my paper on Richard Nixon and the Vietnam War:

Berman, Larry. *No Peace, No Honor: Nixon, Kissinger, and Betrayal in Vietnam.* New York: Free Press, 2001.
Nixon "made it very clear that he did not favor a bombing pause" (27)
He saw bombings as a crucial political tool (27)

Schmitz, David F. *Richard Nixon and the Vietnam War: The End of the American Century.* Lanham, MD.: Rowman & Littlefield, 2014.
America's involvement in Vietnam was part of the U.S.'s larger policy of stopping the spread of communism after WWII (1-2)
U.S. policy officials saw Vietnam's resistance to French control as part of a "larger communist effort" to spread communism (2)
Nixon was an early advocate for U.S. involvement in Vietnam (3)
Before his presidency, Nixon believed "Democrats had not taken necessary measures to win in Vietnam" (11)
He called "for military escalation during the 1964 presidential campaign" (12)

First, I will need to consider merging my notes from my two sources. This will require that I begin to sort my notes into categories.

If you are writing a paper that narrates events in history or explains a process in the order that it happens, you'll want to spend some time organizing your notes on such events or processes into chronological order. If chronology is not a factor in your paper, think through ideas and concepts that you can group your notes into.

For example, if I am writing my paper on Richard Nixon and the Vietnam War in 1968, it might be helpful for me to group my notes by general topics or ideas that I will cover:

- Historical background of Vietnam War
  - ▸ America's involvement in Vietnam was part of the U.S.'s larger policy of stopping the spread of communism after WWII (Schmitz 1-2)
  - ▸ U.S. policy officials saw Vietnam's resistance to French control as part of a "larger communist effort" to spread communism (Schmitz 2)
- Nixon's policies on Vietnam
  - ▸ Nixon was an early advocate for U.S. involvement in Vietnam (Schmitz 3)
  - ▸ Before his presidency, Nixon believed "Democrats had not taken necessary measures to win in Vietnam" (Schmitz 11)
  - ▸ He called "for military escalation during the 1964 presidential campaign" (Schmitz 12)
  - ▸ Nixon "made it very clear that he did not favor a bombing pause" (Berman 27)
  - ▸ He saw bombings as a crucial political tool (Berman 27)

Notice that my notes are no longer organized under the source information. Instead, I've added the author's last name next to the page numbers. This will help me keep track of what source each note is from, so I can still easily cite them when I begin writing. Never forget who wrote what!

These are very broad categories—too broad to stand as main points in my outline. But they function as large buckets I can sort my notes into that will make the process more manageable.

Once your notes are in such "buckets," it might be logical for you to sort your notes chronologically. As I organized my notes under "Nixon's policies on Vietnam," I ordered my notes chronologically. While the notes do not all have specific years associated with them, I knew my notes from Schmitz discussed

Nixon's beliefs in the 1950s and 1960s, and my notes from Berman specifically addressed his opinions during the election of 1968.

Once you've spent some time sifting and ordering your notes, then you can begin the process of grouping your notes by the main points you intend to cover in your paper. Keep in mind that your groupings will ultimately constitute the paragraphs and sections of your paper, so each note sorted under those groupings must be relevant in supporting and explaining that main point. Using my understanding of Nixon's policy beliefs, I would sort those notes as follows:

I. Nixon favored American involvement from the start of the conflict
    A. Nixon was an early advocate for U.S. involvement in Vietnam (Schmitz 3)
    B. Before his presidency, Nixon believed "Democrats had not taken necessary measures to win in Vietnam" (Schmitz 11)
    C. He called "for military escalation during the 1964 presidential campaign" (Schmitz 12)
II. By the election of 1968, Nixon's policies had cemented
    A. Nixon "made it very clear that he did not favor a bombing pause" (Berman 27)
    B. He saw bombings as a crucial political tool (Berman 27)

Notice that my first level statements are specific points that I came up with—they are not notes. I developed these points from my own understanding of my notes and source reading. The notes sorted below the main points provide evidence of or explain those points. Developing your main points requires really thinking through your notes and what you want to say in your paper. It can be hard! It may mean that you need to read through your notes several times before you have a sense of what you want to say. If you need assistance, ask for help from your parent or instructor—they will be happy to help you brainstorm!

You may think that writing is the hardest step in putting a paper together. Actually, that's only true if you haven't organized your notes and thoughts ahead of time—because you then have to organize as you write! Coming up with main points and grouping notes beneath them is the *really* hard part of writing a paper. Do this first, and the actual writing will be painless.

I promise.

By the way: You'll notice in these example outlines that there is no section for "introductions" or "conclusions." That is because an outline is used to organize your notes, which will provide support for the body of your paper. The introduction and conclusion paragraphs require that you have a keen understanding of what the body of the paper will say; therefore, you typically cannot write them until the paper has been drafted.

- Before you begin writing, you must organize your notes.
- An outline helps you organize your notes logically by topic that will later help you organize your paragraphs.
- An outline will typically have two levels: the first level (marked with Roman numerals) is the main idea and the second level (marked with capital letters) includes the notes related to that main topic.
- Long papers may use a third level (marked with numbers) for the notes with the second level indicating subtopics.
- The first step of creating an outline is to bring your notes from your sources together by ordering them either chronologically or by very general categories or subject matter.
- The second step requires grouping your ordered notes by event, step, time frame, or main point.
- How you organize your notes will depend on your paper and requires a great deal of thinking—if you need help, don't be afraid to ask your writing instructor for assistance!

When do I start to write?

As you finish your outline, the flow of thought of your paper should emerge. You can use your main points to establish transitions or develop topic sentences that help connect your groupings together. If there are any "breaks" or "jumps" between your main points, this is the perfect time to return to your sources and take more notes to fill those information gaps. You should also make sure you have at least two notes per grouping so that you have enough detail to explain and support your main points as you start writing.

Once you are happy with the outline, it is time to draft! As I mention in the above section, if you put a good deal of effort into your outline, drafting should be much easier: you are just taking the outlined material and turning it into clear prose.

Keep in mind that the first draft can be rough! I like to remind my students that this is the "sloppy copy"—your goal is just to write all of your ideas out. Try not to get too hung up on your sentences being poetic or your tone being perfect. You can refine and elevate your language in the editing stage.

As you draft, you'll want to begin adding your documentation for the source information (paraphrased or quoted!) that you use in your essay. Even if you do not want to write out the full footnote, endnote, or in-text citation for fear that you will lose your train of thought, be sure to include a place holder with some source information (usually author's last name and page number). You can then efficiently finish your documentation once the draft is complete. Do not wait until you are completely finished with the draft to go back through and add your documentation! While you may be able to easily attribute quotes by looking back at your notes, it will be much more difficult (and time consuming) to try to remember what paraphrased information needs to be cited and what source it came from.

- Before you start writing, read through your outline several times to check the flow of your information.
- As you check your work, you can add transitions to help connect your information.
- If there are any gaps or breaks in the information of your outline, this is the time to go back to your sources and take notes to fill those gaps.
- If you have a thorough outline, drafting will feel easy since you have already planned out your paper's content.
- As you draft, be sure to add your documentation for all borrowed quotes or information that is not common knowledge.

- If you are worried about interrupting the flow of your drafting, be sure to include placeholders for documentation that includes the author's last name and page number.
- Do not ignore documentation now, as it will be more difficult to add later on.

How do I incorporate quotations into my own sentences?

As you write, you want to use the raw material from your notes to highlight the points that you, the writer, are making. You should not simply parrot the ideas that you encounter in the sources. Instead, state your own ideas and conclusions (which the sources have helped you to form) in your own words.

But you should also support those original ideas and conclusions by referring back to your sources. You can do this in two ways: by using **indirect quotations**, or **direct quotations**.

The goal is to use your indirect or direct quotations to support the claims that you are making in your writing. Using my example notes above, I would write the following paragraph:

> Before he won the Presidency in 1968, Nixon solidified his views that increased military force was the only path to winning the Vietnam War. He firmly believed that the Democratic Party "had not taken necessary measures to win in Vietnam," causing him to demand further military action during the 1964 campaign.[1] Historian Larry Berman asserts, "[Nixon] did not favor a bombing pause" well into 1968. Nixon thus knew that calling for increased bombings was a political tool he could use to gain favor with certain voters and politicians.[2]

[1] David F. Schmitz, *Richard Nixon and the Vietnam War: The End of the American Century* (Rowman & Littlefield, 2014), 11, 12.
[2] Larry Berman, *No Peace, No Honor: Nixon, Kissinger, and Betrayal in Vietnam* (Free Press, 2001), 27.

At the start of the paragraph, I assert my central claim: that Nixon's military policy for the Vietnam War was clear before his presidency. I then use both indirect quotes (my paraphrasing of the source information) and direct quotes to support this claim. I have mixed my own paraphrasing of the sources to connect these quotes, and finally end on a summary of Berman's opinion that Nixon viewed military escalation as a political tool.

Indirect quotations

When you incorporate indirect quotes into your drafts, you are consciously taking someone else's ideas or opinions and putting them into your own words. Just be careful not to use too many of the same words as the author—because you'll be inching over towards direct quote at that point!

Direct quotations

When incorporating direct quotations, the goal for using source information is the same, but how you incorporate direct quotations into your writing is much different than how you might use summarized or paraphrased information.

Quotes are wonderful because they allow you to use an author's interesting language or expert opinion in their own words. But because you are using someone else's words, you need to take extra care to connect the language to your own writing and ideas. Otherwise, the quote might sit like a roadblock in your writing, rather than a guardrail for your readers to hang on to.

Here are a few rules you can follow that will help you connect your own writing to the quote. Before we think about how to connect the quote to our writing, let's get some basics out of the way.

1. Quotes should always be surrounded by quotation marks (how else is your reader going to know it's a quote?) and followed by a footnote (we covered this in Part 3, of course).

2. If your quote is a complete sentence, you can keep the first word capitalized, as in the original source.

James Monteith claims, "One of the most valuable discoveries made by Archimedes, the famous scholar of Syracuse, in Sicily, relates to the weight of bodies immersed in water."

3. If you need to remove information from the middle of the quote, to shorten it or because the sentence includes excess information that doesn't relate to your paper, you must use ellipses (. . .) to mark where information has been removed.

    Aaron Burr was a man of great polish and charisma, but "in his political career there was a touch of insincerity, and . . . he used his charm too often to the injury of those women who could not resist his insinuating ways."

The original quote was: "in his political career there was a touch of insincerity, and it can scarcely be denied that he used his charm too often to the injury of those women who could not resist his insinuating ways." But when incorporating it into my sentence, I cut "it can scarcely be denied that"—not because it was unrelated to what I was trying to say, but because the additional phrasing was unnecessary. You can use this tool to help you streamline your quotes so they fit neatly into your sentences.

4. If you are directly quoting the middle of a sentence in your source, you do not need to use ellipses at the beginning or end of the quote to signify that the quote is the middle part of a sentence.

    Catherine the Great "had a certain diffidence of manner at first; but later she bore herself with such instinctive dignity as to make her seem majestic."

This example is correct! What you would NOT want to write is:

Catherine the Great ". . . had a certain diffidence of manner at first; but later she bore herself with such instinctive dignity as to make her seem majestic . . ."

5. Commas should be used to separate the quote from the rest of the sentence or attribution tag.

    The author claims, "Mr. Wilson has long been known as an exquisite master of English prose."

However, if the quote works as a part of the sentence's phrasing or is preceded by "that" then a comma is not needed.

    The author claims that "Mr. Wilson has long been known as an exquisite master of English prose."

Notice how the first example requires a comma because the attribution tag is introducing the quote. But with the addition of "that," the comma is no longer needed because the quote becomes a part of the sentence's phrasing. (In case you're interested, the words *that "Mr. Wilson has long been known as an exquisite master of English prose"* serve as a noun clause, the direct object of the action verb *claims*.)

6. Any punctuation used at the end of the quote (comma, period, question mark, etc.) needs to be inside of the quotation marks.

    In the example above, notice how the final period goes inside the quotation mark at the end. If I reversed the order of the sentence:

    "Mr. Wilson has long been known as an exquisite master of English prose," the author claims.

then the comma also goes inside the final quotation mark.

The only exception to this rule is if you add a question or exclamation mark that was not originally part of the text. In the example below, the writer is incredulous over the author's claim about Mr. Wilson!

> The author claims, "Mr. Wilson has long been known as an exquisite master of English prose"!

In this usage, the author of the quote isn't making an exclamation of his description of Mr. Wilson—he thinks it's completely unexciting. But the author of the essay finds this description unbelievable!

7. Sometimes, you will need to change the spelling of a word or replace a word in the quote for clarity. When doing this, place brackets [ ] around what you have changed.

    > In describing Woodrow Wilson, the author claims that "[he] has long been known as an exquisite master of English prose."

    In this revised version, the phrasing would be repetitive if I used "Mr. Wilson" so I replace the name with a pronoun. The brackets make it clear to my reader that I made a revision to the original quote.

Don't worry about memorizing the above information—you can always double check your work while editing to make sure you are following these formatting rules.

Attribution tags

Now the fun part: bringing your writing and your quotes together!

As mentioned before, your quotes should be used as details to support a claim that you are making in your essay. So you want to make sure you are [1] connecting the quote to your point and [2] explaining what you want your reader to understand from the quote (this may seem obvious to you, but it won't to your reader).

Try thinking of it like a sandwich: if your quote is the delicious filling, your reader needs two slices of bread (connection & explanation) in order to properly eat and digest the information.

Your first slice of bread is your connection. This is your chance to provide some context to the quote; you can do this by attributing the quote to a particular author, by explaining the circumstances in which the quote was spoken or written, or by using your own phrasing to lead up to your quote.

One of the most common ways we do this with **attribution tags** ("she says" or "the author claims"). Attribution tags can come in various forms, so you can use a variety of verbs and phrasings to connect the quote to its author or source. Here are a few examples if you're having trouble coming up with them:

adds	claims	argues	denies	notes
asserts	points out	concludes	explains	shows
states	speculates	illustrates	contends	sees
admits	suggests	defends	compares	writes
believes	emphasizes	implies	observes	maintains

The attribution tag could come before or after a quote, depending on the phrasing:

> The author claims, "Mr. Wilson has long been known as an exquisite master of English prose."

> "Mr. Wilson has long been known as an exquisite master of English prose," the author claims.

The order doesn't matter so much as long as the phrasing of the sentence remains clear. An attribution tag is just one type of bread (say whole wheat), but you can use other types of bread to bring your sandwich together. Sometimes, you may find that instead of using an attribution tag, you are able to paraphrase information in your own words that adequately contextualizes and introduces the quote:

Woodrow Wilson was a profound orator, "known as an exquisite master of English prose" by many.

In my paragraph on Richard Nixon, I use both methods:

He firmly believed that the Democratic Party "had not taken necessary measures to win in Vietnam," causing him to demand further military action during the 1964 campaign.

Historian Larry Berman asserts, "[Nixon] did not favor a bombing pause" well into 1968.

For the first quote, I was able to connect the quote to the larger paragraph with my own introduction. But for the second quote, I used an attribution tag. Both methods work as your first slice of bread, but which one you use will depend on the content of the quote itself.

Your second slice of bread is your explanation of the quote. Even if the quote seems fairly straightforward, you want to spell out why the quote is important or what it shows your reader about your larger point. For example, if I add the following quote to an essay on presidential speeches:

The author claims, "Mr. Wilson has long been known as an exquisite master of English prose."

then I would need to add some explanation linking this piece of information in the quote to the larger point of my paper:

The author claims, "Mr. Wilson has long been known as an exquisite master of English prose." This mastery of oration was a skill Wilson could apply to his speeches, so as to better influence and move his audience.

Ask yourself: what should my reader understand after reading this quote? What do I want my reader to see in this quote? The explanation could be a phrase following the quote, or it could be several sentences long. That will depend on the length of the paper and the quote. But it is essential that you are thorough in your explanation.

For example, here is an excerpt from my analysis of Milton Murayama's book *All I Asking for is My Body:*

> When Kiyo starts his boxing training during the summer he says, "I needed fish or meat . . . I began to hate rice."[1] Since rice is a staple in the Japanese diet, his disdain for rice and craving for red meat is a metaphor for his transition from a Japanese to American identity through his diet.
>
> [1] Milton Murayama, *All I Asking for is My Body* (University of Hawaii Press, 1988), 71.

Before I get to the quote, I provide context of what is happening in the story (he is training every day) and an attribution tag ("he says"). While the quote is fairly straightforward (we understand that he likes one food more than another), what I want the reader to understand from this quote is more complicated. Therefore, I need to spell it out for the reader in a sentence following the quote. I explicitly state that I see Kiyo's statement as a larger metaphor for his changing identity. I would not want to simply write:

> When Kiyo starts his boxing training during the summer he says, "I needed fish or meat . . . I began to hate rice."[1] This shows his changing identity.
>
> [1] Milton Murayama, *All I Asking for is My Body* (University of Hawaii Press, 1988), 71.

This sentence does not fully explain what I want my reader to see in this quote. Instead, I want them to notice the metaphor, but also understand each food as clearly associated with one culture and diet. In spelling that out for the reader, they are able to follow along with my analysis more easily and therefore understand my larger points in the paper.

Adding direct quotes to your writing so that your quotes clearly support your claims and ideas can be difficult. But if you always remember your two slices of bread—context and explanation—your reader will be satisfied with your analysis.

One last word: Whatever you do, NEVER, NEVER, NEVER simply plop a direct quote down in your paper as its own independent sentence! Here is an example of the WRONG way to incorporate a direct quote:

> Kiyo starts his boxing training during the summer. "I needed fish or meat . . . I began to hate rice."[1] Since rice is a staple in the Japanese diet, his disdain for rice and craving for red meat is a metaphor for his transition from a Japanese to American identity through his diet.
>
> [1] Milton Murayama, *All I Asking for is My Body* (University of Hawaii Press, 1988), 71.

Notice how the quote "I needed fish or meat . . . I began to hate rice" just stands on its own? Never do this! Direct quotes *must* be incorporated as part of one of your own sentences.

Block quotes

One last thing to keep in mind when you're using direct quotations!

If a direct quotation is longer than two sentences, indent the entire quote one inch from the margin in a separate block of text and omit quotation marks. You still need the "sandwich" method—an attribution quote and also an explanation! But the quote itself should be separated out from the rest of your own text. If you're using a word processor, double space before and after the quote, like this:

In 1661, the English philosopher Joseph Glanvill predicted the invention of "many things, that are now but Rumors." Among them were space travel, airplanes, and conversation over long distances. In his essay *Scepsis Scientifica,* Glanvill admits that these inventions seem farfetched, but he argues that the discovery of a new continent must have seemed just as unlikely:

> It may be some ages hence, a voyage to the Southern unknown Tracts, yea possibly the Moon, will not be more strange than one to America. To them, that come after us, it may be as ordinary to buy a pair of wings to fly into remotest Regions; as now a pair of Boots to ride a Journey. And to confer at the distance of the Indies by Sympathetick conveyances, may be as usual to future times, as to us in a literary correspondence.[1]

Glanvill goes on to point out that navigating a ship by compass ("the guidance of a Mineral," as he puts it) instead of by the stars must have seemed just as impossible to ancient sailors as moon travel does to people of his own day.

[1] Joseph Glanvill, *Scepsis Scientifica: Or, Confest Ignorance, The Way to Science; In an Essay of the Vanity of Dogmatizing and Confident Opinion* (Paul, Trench & Co., 1885), 157.

The text before and after the quote from Joseph Glanvill was written by Susan Wise Bauer, but Glanvill's own words are set in a block that's indented and separated by double space from the rest of the text—because it's three sentences long.

- The information from the sources can then be used to support your claims and add interesting details and examples.
- Since indirect quotes are your own paraphrasing of a source, you can add them as part of your sentence phrasings as you draft.

- Direct quotes from sources should always be surrounded by quotation marks.
- If your quote is a complete sentence, the first word can be capitalized.
- If you need to remove phrasing from the middle of your quote, you can use ellipses (. . .) to let your readers know that information is missing. But you do not need to use ellipses at the beginning or end of a quote for any reason, even if the quote is from the middle of a sentence.
- Commas should be used to separate the quote from the rest of the sentence, unless the quote has been grammatically incorporated into a sentence.
- Any punctuation at the end of the quote must go inside of the quotation marks. The only exceptions are for question and exclamation marks that were not originally part of the quoted text.
- If you change or revise a word in a quote for clarity, be sure to put the new word in brackets.
- Quotes must always be incorporated into your sentences and should never stand on their own as a sentence in your writing.
- There are two ways to incorporate quotes into sentences: [1] using an attribution tag to link the quote to the source or author or [2] using the quote as a grammatical part of your sentence.
- No matter what, the importance of the quote and how it relates to your larger point must always be spelled out in your writing.

Quick Reference

- Before you begin writing, you must organize your notes.
- An outline helps you organize your notes logically by topic that will later help you organize your paragraphs.
- An outline will typically have two levels: the first level (marked with Roman numerals) is the main idea and the second level (marked with capital letters) includes the notes related to that main topic.
- Long papers may use a third level (marked with numbers) for the notes with the second level indicating subtopics.

- The first step of creating an outline is to bring your notes from your sources together by ordering them either chronologically or by very general categories or subject matter.
- The second step requires grouping your ordered notes by event, step, time frame, or main point.
- How you organize your notes will depend on your paper and requires a great deal of thinking—if you need help, don't be afraid to ask your writing instructor for assistance!
- Before you start writing, read through your outline several times to check the flow of your information.
- As you check your work, you can add transitions to help connect your information.
- If there are any gaps or breaks in the information of your outline, this is the time to go back to your sources and take notes to fill those gaps.
- If you have a thorough outline, drafting will feel easy since you have already planned out your paper's content.
- As you draft, be sure to add your documentation for all borrowed quotes or information that is not common knowledge.
- If you are worried about interrupting the flow of your drafting, be sure to include placeholders for documentation that include the author's last name and page number.
- Do not ignore documentation now, as it will be more difficult to add later on.
- The information from the sources can then be used to support your claims and add interesting details and examples.
- Since indirect quotes are your own paraphrasing of a source, you can add them as part of your sentence phrasings as you draft.
- Direct quotes from sources should always be surrounded by quotation marks.
- If your quote is a complete sentence, the first word can be capitalized.
- If you need to remove phrasing from the middle of your quote, you can use ellipses (. . .) to let your readers know that information is missing.

But you do not need to use ellipses at the beginning or end of a quote for any reason, even if the quote is from the middle of a sentence.

- Commas should be used to separate the quote from the rest of the sentence, unless the quote has been grammatically incorporated into a sentence.
- Any punctuation at the end of the quote must go inside of the quotation marks. The only exceptions are for question and exclamation marks that were not originally part of the quoted text.
- If you change or revise a word in a quote for clarity, be sure to put the new word in brackets.
- Quotes must always be incorporated into your sentences and should never stand on their own as a sentence in your writing.
- There are two ways to incorporate quotes into sentences: [1] using an attribution tag to link the quote to the source or author or [2] using the quote as a grammatical part of your sentence.
- No matter what, the importance of the quote and how it relates to your larger point must always be spelled out in your writing.

CONCLUSION

Now, go write—and cite!

Write carefully, and cite carefully—because facts *matter*.

It's important to find and use good, well-sourced, expert information. It's important to point people to *where* you got that information, so that your readers can check up on *you*. It's important to write down information that is trustworthy, factual, and *true*. It's important to be transparent, open, and honest about where you got that information.

It's important, because truth matters, and honesty matters.

When you write with truth and honesty, your writing will touch a nerve in other people. It will communicate clearly and without deceit. It will encourage your readers to react with openness and clarity. It will start a conversation.

And that is why we write.

INDEX